MATTHEW'S MESSAGE

GOOD NEWS FOR THE NEW MILLENNIUM

GRACE IMATHIU

Abingdon Press
Nashville

Matthew's Message: Good News for the New Millennium

ISBN-10: 0-687-02183-9
ISBN-13: 978-0-687-02183-3
This book is printed on acid-free paper.

Manufactured in the United States of America.

07 08 09 10 11— 15 14 13 12 11

TABLE OF CONTENTS

Meet the Writer

Born and raised on the slopes of Mount Kenya, Grace Imathiu is an ordained minister in the Methodist Church in Kenya and the daughter of a Methodist minister. She is one of the emerging new voices in the Christian world.

Ms. Imathiu is currently pursuing her Ph.D. in New Testament at Vanderbilt University, Nashville, Tennessee.

Ms. Imathiu has enjoyed traveling to many parts of the world leading Bible studies and joining in Christian fellowship with all flavors of God's people. She was a Bible study leader at the Seventeenth World Methodist Conference in 1996 in Rio de Janeiro, Brazil.

A Word of Welcome

Welcome to MATTHEW'S MESSAGE: GOOD NEWS FOR THE NEW MILLENNIUM. We hope you enjoy this fresh new look at the Gospel of Matthew. This six-session study will enrich your understanding of this Gospel and will provide a worthy pursuit of the gospel truth as we approach the third millennium.

This study is thematic; it does not begin with the first chapter of Matthew and proceed through reports of Jesus' ministry to the Resurrection. Rather, the study is organized around six life-oriented questions to help you examine in a renewed way the life and teachings of Jesus.

The Six Questions

At the beginning of the new millennium, many of us have turned our minds to what the new century means for us. The sessions in this study help us with that reflection. Listed in the next column are the questions around which the sessions are organized:

What was Matthew's world like?
What was Matthew's Gospel about?
What does Matthew teach us about the human condition?
What does Matthew teach us about Jesus Christ?
How does Matthew teach us to understand our times?
What does Matthew teach us about living in the third millennium?

Within each lesson there are ample references to the Scriptures that illumine the responses to the question. When possible, we have tried to let Matthew speak to us afresh today.

Studying Matthew Successfully

MATTHEW'S MESSAGE can be used successfully as a self-study or as a group study. Reflection and discussion questions are in boxes at the bottom of the pages throughout the book. The questions refer to information on that page or on an adjacent page.

Use these questions for quiet reflection or as conversation starters. Some of them ask for data: When did something happen? What did Jesus say or do about an event or experience? Others ask for more evaluative responses: Why, do you think, did Jesus treat someone in a particular way? Still other questions personalize the Gospel: What does this ancient teaching mean for you or for the church today?

In each instance, the text will draw you closer into Matthew's world and help you bridge the centuries from the time when Jesus lived and taught to your time, when Jesus' teaching remains alive and vibrant for today.

Reflection Partners

If you are studying Matthew in a group or on your own, you may want a reflection or prayer partner to talk to and pray with during the time between the study sessions. There are more than enough discussion starters to sustain a class; you have more questions to pique your interest than you can cover. You may enjoy pursuing the questions on your own or praying with a partner about the concerns that arise during the study time.

Making a Commitment

You may find during or at the end of your study that you are ready to affirm or reaffirm a commitment of your life to Jesus Christ. We encourage you to reflect carefully on the message Jesus Christ brings to you through the words of Matthew. Do they engage you to grow into a deeper, more complete relationship with God? Do they bring new light to biblical passages that had been unclear or a stumbling block to real understanding?

If you are inspired to a new level of commitment, discuss it with your pastor, your study leader, or a committed friend in the faith. You will find support and welcome.

1

MATTHEW'S WORLD

In most conferences, before a speaker begins her presentation, she is given a personal introduction. Since the audience is often curious to know something more about her and not just about the material being presented, a short introduction usually helps the audience get comfortable with the speaker. The introduction might mention the speaker's areas of expertise and experience with the material and might vouch for her integrity and character. The introduction might also explain any unusual characteristics the speaker might have, such as an accent. Giving her place of birth, for example, explains to the audience why the speaker is different. Though introductions are not part of the formal presentation, they are extremely helpful in situating a speaker.

Unlike the relationship between a speaker and her audience, an author of the written word has a very different relationship with his reader. First of all, the reader and the author are physically separated, and they could also be historically and culturally separated as well. That is to say, the writer might write from a different culture and at a different period in time than the reader. The author is therefore not in a face-to-face situation like the speaker and her audience. In fact the author has no idea who is reading his book! Nevertheless, the reader might be even more curious about the author's identity and credentials.

In modern books, this curiosity is addressed by a very brief biographical sketch of the author on the back cover, which may include a photograph. The brief biographical sketch is often a source of curiosity in itself because, if nothing else, it leaves

How would you describe your cultural setting? How does it affect the way you communicate?

much unanswered. We may still be interested in knowing more about the author; about where he lives (or lived); about his social, economic, political, and cultural circumstances. We may encounter words or ideas unfamiliar to our own context that would be clearer with a more complete understanding of the author and his world. Such an understanding would certainly help us take more seriously the issues raised by an author and even lead us to make helpful and insightful connections with our particular context and lives.

An Oral Tradition

The Gospel of Matthew might make us curious in similar ways. To start with, the Gospel of Matthew was a spoken document long before it was written down. The Gospel assumes the kind of personal knowledge that we find between a speaker and her audience. That is to say, Matthew was very sure whom he was talking to and sure of the particular problems that had to be addressed; therefore he crafted his message in a very particular and specific way.

Second, the Gospel of Matthew became a book when someone, somewhere collected the different accounts, testimonies, and teachings of Jesus and arranged them into an order and into a narrative. The writer of the Gospel of Matthew was not writing his own book the way a novelist writes a novel. The material he had was not his own original material that he fabricated. The writer of Matthew was a collector who was putting into writing a Gospel that was already known to the Christians in his town or village and that was passed from one hearer to the next, mostly by word of mouth. So, the first Christians probably already knew many, many accounts, stories, sayings, and teachings about Jesus. Putting down in a book form the account of Jesus must have been a tremendous task. Someone had to choose the stories that were to be recorded; for, as John says, "there are also many other things that Jesus did; if every one of them was written down, I suppose that the world itself could not contain the books that would be written" (John 21:25). Accounts were chosen perhaps because they were best-loved stories, or they had a teaching for the situation the church or believers were in, or they made the point of who Jesus was.

What stories has your family passed along?

What are your favorites? Why?

Since this Gospel was written without benefit of immediately recorded notes, it includes fragments of testimonies of Jesus' teachings and deeds from the people who had been healed, from their relatives, from the disciples and the crowds who followed Jesus. Since much had happened since the time of Jesus' physical departure, some of these witness accounts were told and retold and passed on by second- and third-generation believers. Perhaps some accounts were written in a letter or documented by a group of believers.

Even within the Gospel itself we learn that the news of Jesus is transmitted through word of mouth (Matthew 4:23-25; 9:31; 14:34-36). It is possible that this might at first raise for us some fears, especially when details tend to get either lost or confused when passed from one hearer to the next. Indeed, some details got lost in the transmission. For instance, it seems that on occasion names of people were either forgotten or were confused with someone else. But we need not be too worried about the big picture. Whatever happened between the time of Jesus' earthly life and the writing of the book, we know that the accounts of Jesus were kept alive by being retold in a community of believers.

The Development of the Scriptures

The Gospel of Matthew, then, was not a book during its earliest or "original" form. The early Christians did not have a special book of their own the way we have the New Testament as the special book of Christians. The early Christians used the same Hebrew Scriptures (which we call the Old Testament) that were used in the synagogue. Since most of these Christians lived in a time when Greek was the main language, the Hebrew Scriptures had been translated into Greek and were called the *Septuagint.*

In addition to the Old Testament, the early Christians also used the testimonies, witnesses, and accounts of Jesus that they shared with one another. We might compare the Scriptures, including Matthew, to the hymn-book in many of our churches. Although a gifted musician might be responsible for gathering, arranging, and even editing the words and music, the finished product belongs to the community.

Living two millennia later and more removed from the actual events of Jesus Messiah's earthly ministry, Christians today can

What historical stories ought to be kept alive? Why?

only be grateful for Matthew's recording of some of the accounts that were well-known to the early Christians. Since Matthew was not consciously writing "a book," the original manuscript did not have a title. Matthew's intention was to record the accounts of Jesus that were already known to his community in a way that gave the message of Jesus for the church. The title "The Gospel According to Matthew" was added much later as a way of distinguishing this particular Gospel from Luke, Mark, John, and other gospels that have not been included in the New Testament.

Therefore if we are to ask who was the particular person responsible for writing the Gospel of Matthew, it would be a hopeless investigation. We can see that there was not a single individual who "composed" the Gospel in the way a bestseller is composed. We have seen that Matthew was a collector of accounts that already existed and also a theologian who arranged these accounts into a narrative that has a beginning, an ending, and a message.

The Gospel of Matthew is first and foremost a religious text. Its primary intention is to communicate a particular faith. Matthew's Gospel is not a disinterested and objective report about Jesus, his life, mission, and passion. Matthew has convictions about who Jesus is; Matthew has commitments toward living the life of discipleship; and Matthew tells us he has been charged to communicate and spread the good news (28:18-20).

The Purpose and Writing of Matthew

Matthew gathered all these accounts and wrote them in his Gospel around A.D. 85 to 90. In the Gospel of Matthew we not only have the accounts of Jesus, we also see Matthew's strong familiarity with and attention to the Hebrew Scriptures. Matthew, for instance, continues many of the major themes in the Old Testament—covenant, blessing, curses, inheritance, and law.

Matthew goes further and shows a great concern about how the church fits into the story of Israel that is told in the Scriptures. In this way, Matthew is exceptional and quotes the Old Testament more than any of the other Gospels. But Matthew was more than a collector of quotations and stories; he was also a theologian who arranged these many varied

What is for you the most significant passage in this Gospel?

What is your conviction about Jesus? How is this good news for you?

accounts of Jesus to make a certain pattern or message. Matthew was like an artist who takes different colored and shaped beads and strings them together to make a wonderful necklace that has a beginning, an ending, and a pattern.

In his quotations, Matthew is especially interested in showing the fulfillment of God's promises in Jesus; Jesus is the Messiah whom the prophets spoke about. Therefore Matthew continually says, "This was to fulfill what the Lord had spoken by the prophet." The events surrounding the birth of Jesus fulfill what "has been written by the prophet" (Matthew: 2:3), and Jesus is a refugee in Egypt "to fulfill what had been spoken by the Lord through the prophet" (2:15). Jesus therefore did not come "to abolish but to fulfill" the law (5:17).

After reading Matthew from beginning to end, we know clearly that Jesus as Messiah was the fulfillment of God's promise and brought in a new order and epoch of history. The church as the radically different community founded by Jesus Messiah has strong bonds and claims in the history, the promises, and the traditions of Israel.

As a religious text Matthew attempts to communicate a particular way of understanding God's will and therefore of living life in obedience to God's will. As a religious text of a believing community, Matthew also intends to strengthen and encourage the faith of the believers as well as to correct and instruct the believers. Matthew is the only Gospel that uses the word *church* (16:18; 18:15, 17), and his Gospel intends to establish the meaning and identity of the individual Christian as well as the community of believers known as the church.

Recording the Master Teacher

Of all the Gospels in our New Testament, Matthew's Gospel is by far the longest. This is mostly due to the fact that this Gospel has material that the other Gospels do not have. When we

In what ways do you see plans and promises fulfilled by God in your life?

Look up Matthew 2:3-15. What else does this passage tell you about Jesus?

How do you recognize God's will? What encouragement do you receive to live in God's will?

read the Gospels side by side and compare their content, the Gospel of Matthew contains most of Mark's stories and teachings and also has additional material that is not found in Mark. Most scholars believe that the Gospel of Mark was the first Gospel to be written and that Matthew had a copy of Mark when he wrote his Gospel. If this is true, perhaps there were those in Matthew's church who remembered other teachings and events of Jesus Messiah. Or perhaps as the first-generation Christians aged and died, Matthew's church had begun documenting material that was not documented by Mark. Papias, a church historian at the beginning of the second century, tells us that "Matthew collected the sayings of Jesus in the Hebrew language."

Jesus was a master teacher who taught using memorable stories in the form of parables. If nothing else, we know from personal experience that although we might forget Sunday's sermon, we will often remember a story the preacher gave—especially if it was a story that was surprising, funny, or had an unexpected ending. What is more interesting about such stories is that we might not be comfortable sharing the content of the sermon in our workplace; but often enough, if the story is quick-witted, we will pass it on even among our non-believing friends. Parables are exactly that.

Parables are short stories; parables have an unexpected twist; parables are surprising; parables are memorable; parables get passed on. The parables of Jesus have survived two millennia and are still going strong!

Jesus, the teacher par excellence, taught using short, attention-catching, and fresh sayings. Like the parables, these sayings were also easy to remember and pass on. Who can forget Jesus saying that "you strain out a gnat but swallow a camel" (Matthew 23:24)? If we are not the ones being referred to, the image is quite funny. We can probably think of someone who, for the sake of tradition, gets mean-

If you have a Bible or a reference work that compares Matthew with Mark, scan it to see how much of Mark is included in Matthew. What do you think is the significance of this?

What is one of the principal teaching/speaking tools employed by Jesus?

How are parables effective? What biblical parables have been particularly effective for you? What modern parables?

spirited over some trivial detail such as washing hands before eating a meal, but who also uses the same tradition to justify breaking God's commandment by dishonoring mother and father (15:1-9).

Some of the sayings of Jesus are so popular that they have become part of the modern pop culture. I have on occasion heard the sayings of Jesus used in ordinary conversation that was not particularly religious. When faced with a decision to leave an ignorant or dull group, we do well to remember to "let the dead bury their own dead" (8:22). And when under peer pressure to vote for corrupt leaders or to flirt with dangerously addictive pleasure, we do well to heed the advice that "the gate is wide and the road is easy that leads to destruction" (7:13).

Even those of us who have the worst memories can remember Jesus' teachings by recalling these short, pithy sayings. Through witty and biting images, Jesus' teachings can be passed on to others even by those who are most reluctant about sharing the good news outside the church! In addition to being short and witty, these sayings carry truths about life, and we can relate to them as indeed true.

Who among us has not seen people who pretend to be kind but turn out to be "ravenous wolves" "in sheep's clothing" (7:15). On the other hand, you can see how these saying can be provocative. No one likes to be referred to as a wolf in sheep's clothing or as the dead! Those to whom Jesus was referring could hardly have appreciated it, especially if these teachings were given in a form that people remembered and told to others. No wonder Jesus collected some very angry enemies! Such is a commitment to the truth.

Who Is Matthew?

Matthew is committed to telling the truth about Jesus. Matthew is more than a historian, more than a writer, more than an author, more than an editor or a scribe. Matthew can be more accurately described as an evangelist who is pooling together a variety of traditions and witnesses and parables

How do Jesus' sayings strike home? Read Matthew 23:24-36.

Read Matthew 15:1-9. How can the letter of the law be used to circumvent the spirit of the law? What other examples can you think of?

Read Matthew 8:22; 7:13, 15. What do these comments mean in context? mean to you?

and sayings to produce a religious text for a missionary-minded church.

Among the special Matthew material is the story of Matthew's call by Jesus. Jesus was walking along (in the same manner he had walked along when he had seen Peter and the other fishermen) and "he saw a man called Matthew sitting at the tax booth; and he said to him, 'Follow me' " (9:9). By being in his tax booth, Matthew was unmistakably identified as an employed tax collector. Yet there is no report of a conversation between Jesus and Matthew, and even more surprising, no report of a conversion experience in Matthew. Jesus simply sees Matthew and calls him, saying, "Follow me." Matthew gets up, leaves his tax booth, and follows Jesus, an event sure to surprise, if not offend, almost any Jew.

Matthew's former occupation was cause for great concern. Not only were tax collectors seen as backstabbers because they were Jews who were in the employment of the hated colonial government of Rome, they were also seen as greedy, dishonest, and corrupt. Rome had given tax collectors the elbow room to decide how much tax to charge as long as they gave the expected assessment of their region to the Roman government. Often enough, tax collectors asked for amounts that were comparable to outrageous kickbacks. When Zacchaeus the tax collector gave his shocking confession, one wonders if half of his possessions had been acquired using dishonest means (Luke 19:1-10).

The general strained animosity toward tax collectors was understandable. The community in turn penalized tax collectors by excluding them from social gatherings. In fact, the social exclusion of tax collectors became an illustration of how persistent wrongdoers in the community were to be treated (see Matthew 18:15-17).

Matthew the tax collector was very different from the first disciples, Peter, Andrew, James, and John, who had also been called while they were working

Read about Matthew's call in Matthew 9:9. Have you ever perceived God calling you to something? What did you do?

Look up "tax collector" in a Bible dictionary. What were they like? Why were they so particularly scorned and shunned?

Review Matthew 18:15-17. What is the point of this story? What does it mean to you?

(4:18-22). Perhaps we would expect that fishermen made their living in the hard, honest, self-employed work of fishing, unlike tax collectors who swindled other people out of their hard-earned money. The unexpected and radical call of a tax collector can be understood more clearly by recognizing how greatly despised tax collectors were. Therefore, Jesus' call of Matthew, the tax collector, is a radical act that turns the common view of tax collectors on its head.

The new community the Messiah ushers in is radical in its composition. It is a community of mercy and restoration. Despite Jesus seeing Matthew "sitting at the tax booth," Jesus did not condemn Matthew but showed him mercy by giving him the chance to "follow me" (9:9). And he did. It is therefore stirring to hear Matthew the tax collector's name in the roll call of the twelve disciples and see this previously excluded man participate in the new community of Jesus Messiah (10:1-4). Tradition has honored him by delegating this Gospel to carry his name.

Matthew's Community of Believers

In addition to asking who the individual Matthew was, we might investigate the community of believers behind the production of the Gospel of Matthew. To make a long and complex history short and simple, we can pinpoint A.D. 70 as a turning point. That year Jerusalem fell and the Temple was destroyed by the Romans. The experience was theologically shattering for the faithful and a traumatic cultural blow for everyone, Jews and Gentiles alike. The immediate question for the faithful was how to understand what it meant to be faithful to God without the Temple and its related political institutions.

For Jews, it meant that the promises relating to the Temple had to be looked at afresh. This began under the leadership of Johanan ben Zakkai at the city of Javneh. There was a major reformation of Judaism to cope with this radically new situation. Much of the Jewish literature from this period tries to envision the will of God for Judaism in these new circumstances and to propose mean-

How is Matthew's call different from that of the first four disciples?

What to you is the significance of Jesus' call of Matthew?

Look up *temple* in a Bible dictionary. What is the significance of the Temple? of its destruction?

ing and action for the faithful community.

In the Christian circles, similar shock waves were experienced theologically and culturally. Matthew's church had to struggle with what it meant to interpret these new circumstances through Jesus Messiah. Although the Jewish communities of Matthew (in Syrian Antioch) and of Javneh were struggling with the same crisis, gradually the theological distance between Javneh and Antioch became too divergent for fellowship. By the time Matthew was written, it seems that the Christians had begun to be excluded from the synagogues (4:23; 9:35; 12:9).

When we read Matthew, we might be taken aback that although Matthew is a Jewish Christian, he expresses seemingly strong sentiments against Jewish leaders (Matthew 23). These sentiments might be particularly unsettling for us today as we look back and see how church history has disgracefully figured among the persecutors of Jews. This persecution is all the more shameful for the Gentile church because God's promise was fulfilled through Jewish theology and history. We would therefore expect Gentile Christians to have shown a certain gratitude toward Judaism, not hostility.

As we study Matthew, we need to keep firmly in mind that Christianity began as an offshoot of first-century Judaism. After all, Jesus was born a Jew in Jewish history; Matthew was a Jew; and the Pharisees were Jews. Unlike our predominantly Gentile Christianity, much of the tension between the first Christians and Judaism was a family dispute. This means that modern Gentile Christians must be particularly attentive and careful about jumping into a family quarrel. Of course as Christians we have a theological and spiritual kinship with Matthew who proclaims Jesus as Messiah. It is understandable for us to take a stand with Matthew, but before we do it is just as critical to understand Matthew's position in his quarrel with Judaism.

Look up Matthew 4:23; 9:35; 12:9. What is the relationship between Jesus and his followers and the Temple community?

Look up Matthew 23. What does it reveal about Matthew's sentiments concerning Jewish leaders?

Do you see current evidence of a quarrel of Christians with Judaism? If so, what form does it take? What can be done about it?

The Antioch Church

Although we do not have total consensus, most scholars conclude that the evangelist Matthew and his church were Jewish Christians who lived in the city of Antioch. Using the Acts of the Apostles as one of our resources, we see that Christianity was brought to Antioch by a Jewish Christian community who for quite some time preached the good news only to other Jews. These Jewish Christians had fled Jerusalem after the stoning of Stephen. In Acts 8:1, we learn that "severe persecution began against the church in Jerusalem, and all except the apostles were scattered throughout the countryside of Judea and Samaria." Acts 11:19 continues the story telling us that "those who were scattered because of the persecution that took place over Stephen traveled as far as Phoenicia, Cyprus, and Antioch, and they spoke the word to no one except Jews."

When believers from Cyprus and Cyrene began to preach the good news of the Lord Jesus in Antioch, many Greek speakers were converted; and the church in Antioch began to grow in numbers and in ethnic diversity. Reports of the growing church reached the apostles in Jerusalem who sent Barnabas to see what was going on in Antioch. Barnabas rejoiced at the work and devotion of the believers in Antioch, then traveled to Tarsus and brought Saul back to Antioch. With Saul, Barnabas taught and preached in Antioch for an entire year. As Gentiles converted, the Greek-speaking Jewish Christians made a momentous decision to accept convert Gentiles without requiring circumcision. Antioch was the city where these radical followers of Jesus received the new name "Christians," which has stuck (Acts 11:26). I suppose it is sort of like Methodists being teased with a name that stuck!

The Fulfillment of Promise

As Matthew's church remembered and retold the teachings and accounts of Jesus, it became clearer and clearer to them that the person and work of Jesus of Nazareth had already fulfilled God's work in Israel's history. The Messiah had already come, fulfilled Judaism, predicted the destruction of Jerusalem, and ush-

Find Antioch of Syria on a map of the first-century Middle East. How far did the persecuted Christians travel?

How would you describe the growth in ethnic diversity in the early church?

ered in a new and radically different community (Matthew 1:22; 2:15, 17, 23; 5:17; 24:1-2). This new Jesus community reflected a continuity of God's work in history (1:1); in the covenant, the Law (5:18-20); in the promises, and in the mercy and judgment of God (9:13; 3:12).

The new Jesus community also showed God's power to create a new people that included both the previously excluded—sinners and Gentiles (3:9; 8:11-12). Furthermore, God's judgment was no longer just limited to Judaism but had opened its doors and was universal (25:32; 28:19).

Reading Matthew's Gospel makes it imperative for us to read within the context of a community of believers that is firmly rooted in "the genealogy of Jesus the Messiah, the son of David, the son of Abraham" (1:1), the son of God (1:20), who teaches and commissions and is forever present among the witnessing work of his disciples to all nations (28:20).

We have seen that the Gospel of Matthew was already being lived out by a community of believers in the first century before it was written down in the form of a book. In other words, the church came into being before the special books of the church collected in the New Testament were put together. Although the first Christians do not make any such claim, two millennia later we cannot help admiring them because God's law was written in their hearts. The community of believers who lived their lives as reflected in the Gospel of Matthew had convictions. They saw life and history and themselves with the eyes of faith. They understood their identity as shaped by the promise that God had fulfilled in the story of Jesus Messiah.

Review these passages (1:22; 2:15, 17, 23; 5:17; 24:1-2). How do they describe the community?

Who is included? excluded? Read these four passages (3:9; 8:11-12; 25:32; 28:19).

How does Matthew describe Jesus and his purpose? Review Matthew 1:1, 20; 28:20. What does this mean to you?

How do you understand your identity as a Christian? Take a moment in prayer to dedicate or rededicate your commitment to follow Christ.

MATTHEW'S MESSAGE

MATTHEW TELLS HIS STORY

One of the ways to describe the way each of our lives unfolds is as a story or a narrative. When we look back, the single, separate events of our lives can be threaded together into a narrative. Perhaps we are most aware of this at funerals and memorial services when the eulogy is read; and from our loved one's accomplishments, successes, and failures, we hear a coherent and purposeful narrative.

In the same way, the Gospel of Matthew records the life of Jesus of Nazareth as a coherent and purposeful narrative. Therefore first and foremost, Matthew's Gospel is the story of Jesus, which begins with the ancestry of Jesus (1:1-17), continues to Jesus' birth and childhood (1:18–2:23), bap-

tism (3:1-17), ministry (4:1–26:2), passion (26:3–27:66), resurrection (28:1-15), and finally to his commission to his followers (28:16-20). The largest portion of Matthew's Gospel is devoted to the ministry of Jesus.

More than any other Gospel, Matthew includes the direct teachings, speeches, lectures, and parables of Jesus. If you rapidly look through the different Gospels in a Bible that records the words of Jesus in red letters, you will be aware of the great frequency as well as the length of red sections in Matthew.

Easy to Remember

In addition to using a story format to guide us through the life of

Who writes the eulogies? How is the narrative of one's life chosen? In which ways do we write our own stories? Whose stories do we remember at family gatherings? Skim the first two chapters of each Gospel. At what point of his life do the other Gospels begin their story of Jesus?

Read Luke 24:50-53 and Matthew 28:16-20. How is Luke's epilogue different from Matthew's?

Jesus, the material of Matthew's Gospel is divided and arranged in a very particular order. Some scholars have suggested that Matthew has arranged his material in a way that makes it possible to memorize the entire Gospel quite easily. This is especially true of the large central section that lies between the birth narrative and the Passion narrative and takes more than three-quarters of the Gospel. In this section we find Matthew repeating the phrase "when Jesus had finished." This phrase is repeated five times (Matthew 7:28; 11:1; 13:53; 19:1; 26:1). The phrase has been understood to be a formula that provides a clue to one possible way to divide the material. Some scholars use this phrase as a signal for the end of one book in Matthew and the beginning of another. In this way the rather bulky and dense material in Matthew's midsection becomes easily accessible into five "addresses" or "books." The first two chapters are seen as a preamble and the final chapters as an epilogue.

Five Books

The idea of five books is especially important for Matthew's Jewish background in the Hebrew Scriptures. The Hebrew Scriptures place a special emphasis on the first five books, which contain the Torah. In the Torah (commonly translated as "law") we find mainly instructions and teachings for the community of God's people. The Torah was given as an act of God's supreme love because it was the way to know God's will.

Most of the Torah was given to Moses on a mountain at Sinai and then taught to the Israelites. There are parallels between Matthew and the Torah. Matthew sees his Gospel as an act of God's supreme love because it is the way to know God's will. Jesus, who is the fulfillment of God's promise, gives the church—as the new community of God's people—instructions and teachings so they can know and do the will of God. The church in turn is to teach the entire world (28:20).

This important teaching man-

As we come to the end of the second millennium and begin a third millennium, the phrase "when Jesus had finished" holds a special meaning. What has finished with the second millennium? What has not yet finished?

What do you know about the Law (for example, the Ten Commandments)? How is Jesus' teaching similar?

ual for the early church can be arranged into seven sections:

- Preamble: Matthew 1–2
- Book One—Radical Discipleship: Matthew 3:1–7:29
- Book Two—Mission: Matthew 8:1–11:1
- Book Three—Kingdom of Heaven: Matthew 11:2–13:53
- Book Four—Community: Matthew 13:54–19:1
- Book Five—Judgment: Matthew 19:2–26:1
- Epilogue: Matthew 26:2–28:20

The Preamble: Matthew 1–2

For anyone who has never heard of the Jesus story, the Gospel of Matthew is a good Gospel to begin with because it begins from scratch with the Jesus story and concludes with the Great Commission. In the opening verse Matthew tells us clearly that he is writing "an account of the genealogy of Jesus the Messiah" (1:1). Matthew does not understand Jesus' history as beginning with his birth. Matthew reaches way back into the salvation story of Israel to situate Jesus' historical account. Matthew connects Jesus to the entire story of God's salvation that is told in Israel's history.

Therefore the story of Jesus can only be understood as part and parcel of Israel's history of salvation. The story of Jesus is a continuation of the salvation history that is told in Israel's story. Of most significance is that the story of Jesus is a fulfillment of the story of Israel.

Matthew begins by introducing Jesus as "son of David, the son of Abraham" (1:1). Matthew places Jesus firmly in the royal Davidic bloodline as "son of David" and also as a Hebrew by his relationship to Abraham as "the son of Abraham." But Matthew is full of surprises and does not spare any blushes.

At the very beginning of his Gospel, Matthew surprisingly includes five women in the genealogy of Jesus Messiah: Tamar (1:3), Rahab (1:5), Ruth (1:5), the wife of Uriah (1:6), and Mary (1:16). These women are similar in some ways and different in others. They all are removed from positions of power and are socially marginalized as women. One is unmarried, one is a prostitute, and three are widowed. What a combination! More surprisingly two of these women, Ruth and Rahab, are Gentiles.

In a way Matthew is washing the dirty laundry of Israelite

Using a Bible dictionary, look up each of these five women (Tamar, Rahab, Ruth, the wife of Uriah, Mary). What more do you learn about them? How do they seem significant for Jesus' story?

ancestry in public. The inclusion of Gentiles in Jesus' ancestry begins very early in the Gospel of Matthew. Nevertheless, these women display a certain radical trait of discipleship: each of these women was agent to furthering the divine purpose and acted in radical ways that were unexpected by the social mores of her time.

Book One: Matthew 3:1–7:29 The Call to Radical Discipleship and Higher Righteousness

Now when Jesus had finished saying these things, the crowds were astounded at his teaching, for he taught them as one having authority and not as their scribes (7:28-29).

This first book contains both narrative and discourse and establishes the authority of Jesus. The narrative includes baptism, temptation, preaching, and calling of disciples. The public ministry of Jesus Messiah begins with the arrest of John. Jesus proclaims the identical message of John the Baptist, "Repent, for the kingdom of heaven has come near" (compare 3:1-2 and 4:17).

As he walks by the Sea of Galilee preaching, Jesus begins to call disciples. His first disciples are two pairs of brothers who are fishermen. Jesus sees them, calls them, and they immediately leave what they are doing to follow him. They obey Jesus' call.

In this book we see Jesus being obedient to God by seeking to live in God's will. Jesus therefore seeks to be baptized by John to fulfill all righteousness (3:13-17). Jesus makes a conscious decision. Jesus initiates the action. When John the Baptist hesitates, Jesus invites John to put aside his reservations and to bend to God's will. Jesus calls John the Baptist to be obedient by performing the baptism.

Look up Matthew 3:1-2 and 4:17. Who is speaking? What does it mean to repent? Of what do you need to repent to prepare for the Kingdom?

Read 3:13-17. The baptism leaves no doubt of Jesus as God's son, the Beloved. What is being challenged by the devil in the temptation story? What is the nature of sonship that Jesus displays? How does the temptation story show Jesus' obedience to God?

How do you feel that God has called you, and what do you perceive as God's will for you? How do you live in order to "fulfill all righteousness"?

To fulfill all righteousness is to live in a way that is in agreement with God's will and well-pleasing to God. Righteousness is not a step toward the kingdom of heaven but the very substance of the Kingdom. Those who hunger for righteousness, who are persecuted for righteousness, are declared blessed (5:6, 10). The citizens of the kingdom of heaven have a righteousness that exceeds that of religious authorities (6:1-2). Yet righteousness is a gift that comes from striving for the kingdom of God (6:33). The necessity of obedience is exemplified by the metaphor of the good tree bearing good fruit (7:17-20). False prophets who are not citizens of the kingdom of heaven are therefore exposed by their inability to bear good fruit.

The discourse in the form of the Sermon on the Mount fills most of Book One (3:1–7:29). Jesus delivers a major section of this book from a mountain, which echoes Moses on Mount Sinai and underlines the authority of the instructions. The Sermon on the Mount has been claimed as the heart and center of Christian faith and as a new ethic for the world.

A large portion of the Sermon is taken up with interpretation of the Law (5:17-48). Jesus clarifies that he has not come to abolish the Law but to fulfill it (5:17). Jesus therefore demands that his followers keep the Law; but more than that, they should check the beginnings of lawbreaking behavior. Therefore, although the Law forbids murder, the new community is to guard against anger (5:21-26). The Law forbids adultery, but the new community is to check lustful desire (5:27-30). The Law forbids divorce, but the new community is to check unfaithfulness (5:31-32). The Law forbids swearing falsely, but the new community is not to swear at all (5:33-37). The Law allows proportional retaliation of tit for tat, but the new community is to turn the other cheek (5:38-42). The Law allows hatred for enemies, but the new community is to love abundantly and to pray for persecutors (5:43-48).

Book Two: Matthew 8:1–11:1 Claiming the Mission as Witnesses of the Gospel

Now when Jesus had finished instructing his twelve disciples, he went on from there to teach and proclaim his message in their cities (11:1).

Divide the Sermon on the Mount, according to the paragraph breaks in your Bible, among the group members. What are the various teachings? How does the entire discourse inform and influence your own ministry and concept of personal discipleship?

This second book contains both narrative and discourse as does the first book. One of the main features of this book is the record of the first mission trip of the Twelve (10:5-42). Scholars have noted that very little is mentioned about the content of the disciples' proclamation. Instead, Jesus emphasizes the lifestyle and activity of his disciples. They are to "cure the sick, raise the dead, cleanse the lepers, cast out demons" (10:8). They are to have only very basic possessions (10:9-10) and to depend on the hospitality of strangers (10:11-15). They are to understand themselves as ambassadors of the one who has sent them (10:40) and to be assured of God's presence with them (10:19-20, 26).

Unlike the first book, this second book contains characters. We are suddenly overwhelmed by the number of people who pop in and out of the Gospel! Although the first book had hinted at the presence of the sick and the crowds around Jesus (4:23-25), we meet them personally in the second book; and the Gospel takes on the features of a walk-in clinic!

With the exception of the disciples, none of these characters is named. They are introduced by their need (9:2, 27), by their relationship (8:14; 9:18), or by their work or position (8:5-13; 9:18). They spend only a few verses with us and disappear never to be heard of again. Only the twelve disciples are named (10:2-4). Although the characters therefore remain anonymous, the reason for their encounter with Jesus is all the more emphasized and remembered; and their situations become the occasion for their encounter with Jesus.

In this second book of the new community created around Jesus, we meet a leper (8:2); a centurion (8:5); Peter's mother-in-law (8:14); would-be followers of Jesus (8:18); two demon-possessed men (8:28); a paralyzed man (9:2); a tax collector named Matthew (9:9); the disciples of John (9:14); Jairus and his daughter (9:18); a hemorrhaging woman (9:20); two blind men (9:27); a mute, demon-possessed man (9:32); and the

Review the mission trip. What are the disciples' instructions? Look especially at three themes: to have no fear, the cost of discipleship, and the reward for hospitality. How easily can you follow these teachings and commissions? Explain.

Look up some of the characters in the second and third paragraphs above. Who are they? What is their role in the Gospel story? What, do you think, is your role?

twelve disciples (10:2-4). With these people, we receive an introductory sample of the unusual mix of people that begins to make up the new community of God's people gathered around Jesus. They are not a uniform band. They range from Roman soldiers to synagogue leaders; from powerless, bleeding women to those who were once blind but whose sight is restored. They are all recipients of God's grace; hence we would expect them to be generous in demonstrating God's grace to others.

Book Three:
Matthew 11:2–13:53
The Nature of the
Kingdom of Heaven

When Jesus had finished these parables, he left that place (13:53).

According to the previous verse (11:1), this third book is taught in the cities. This third book contains wonderful stories in the form of parables. Parables are short stories that use ordinary imagery to point to a real but mysterious reality that is difficult to articulate. There are indeed some mysteries in life that can only be described using a parable.

Take, for instance, love. Love is our best known and most sought after gift. When we listen to the radio, it seems that every song is about love. But in spite of being quite a common human experience, love is the most difficult human experience to describe. King Solomon counted falling in love as among the four wonders of the world (Proverbs 30:19).

The kingdom of heaven likewise is mysteriously present among us but difficult to articulate. Jesus used parable after parable to give clues about the nature of the kingdom of heaven. Among the insights, we can see that the kingdom of heaven is surprisingly among us in the natural world. This is quite different from the idea many might have of the kingdom of heaven as being so completely Other that it is beyond recognition. Jesus compares the Kingdom to trees bearing fruit (12:33-37), to seeds growing (13:1-9), to weeds among wheat (13:24-30), to the tiniest of the seeds growing up to be the biggest tree that becomes a home for the birds of the air

Look up some of the characters in the paragraph beginning "In this second book." What do they do? What do they want? How are they like characters for all time? How are they like you?

Look up "kingdom of heaven" in a Bible dictionary. What is the Kingdom like?

(13:31-32), and to yeast (13:33).

The listeners to the parables are like different soils that receive seeds in different ways (13:3-23). Some soils are inhospitable; some soils are careless; some soils are ill-equipped; but some soils are hospitable and nurturing so that they bear fruit—thirty, sixty, and one-hundredfold (13:23).

For Matthew, the truth of the kingdom of heaven is seen in the fruit-bearing of those who follow. Therefore the kingdom of heaven is not something readily understood by all. Instead, only those who have special understanding of what is valuable and what is not—the "connoisseurs" of treasures, of pearls, of wheat, of fish—know the worth of the Kingdom. These know that the Kingdom is a treasure worth selling everything for (13:44-50).

Book Four: Matthew 13:54–19:1
The Church in Community

When Jesus had finished saying these things, he left Galilee and went to the region of Judea beyond the Jordan (19:1).
Book Four begins in Jesus' home-town of Nazareth where he is rejected. The book contains narrative and notable dialogue between Jesus and a variety of people. We overhear conversations between Jesus and his disciples (14:15-19; 15:12-20, 32-36; 16:5-12, 13-14; 17:9-13, 19-22; 18:1-5), with Peter (14:25-33; 16:15-19, 22-23; 17:24-27; 18:21-22), with a Canaanite woman (15:21-28), with the Pharisees (15:1-9; 16:1-4), and with the Sadducees (16:1-4). This book contains the Transfiguration and vision of Moses and Elijah with Jesus (17:1-8); two predictions of Jesus' death and resurrection (16:21-23; 17:22-23); the story of John the Baptist's death (14:1-12), which foreshadows the violent passion and the resurrection of Jesus; the first prediction of the Passion and the Resurrection (16:21-28); the second prediction of the Passion and the Resurrection (17:22-23).

This book also contains two feeding stories. In one story Jesus feeds about "five thousand men, besides women and children" (14:21) with five loaves of bread and two fish (14:13-21). Jesus

Review these parables of the Kingdom (Matthew 13:24-33, 44-50). What contemporary images might we use today? How do you recognize signs of the Kingdom?

Look up the two feeding stories (Matthew 14:13-21 and 15:32-39) in the Bible and in a commentary. How is this miracle explained? How would you explain it? How does it compare to what we do during Communion?

takes bread, gives thanks, breaks it, and gives it to his disciples who give it to the crowd (14:19). After everyone has had enough to eat, twelve baskets full are left over. It is not readily clear whether these baskets are symbolic and represent the twelve tribes of Israel or if each of the twelve disciples gathered a basket full of abundance.

In the second story, Jesus feeds "four thousand men, besides women and children" (15:38) with only seven loaves and a few fish. Jesus takes bread and fish, repeats the thanksgiving formula, so familiar to us now as the Communion liturgy, and the disciples offer the meal to the crowd (15:36). Seven baskets full are left over after everyone has had enough to eat.

The feeding stories are set in geographical places where those who have come to hear Jesus cannot find anything to eat. Like the children of Israel in the wilderness, the Jesus community is fed with bread by God's Son. As we enter the new millennium, these two stories become particularly important for our journey through places of wilderness. Our feeding story is the final act of Jesus, who took bread and the cup, broke it, and gave it to us as his body and blood of a new covenant (26:26-29).

> **The new community of God's people is called to rejoice, especially when our neighbors are the recipients of God's generosity.**

Book Five: Matthew 19:2–26:1 Judgment

When Jesus had finished saying all these things, he said to his disciples, "You know that after two days the Passover is coming, and the Son of Man will be handed over to be crucified" (26:1-2).

In the fifth book Jesus enters Jerusalem and predicts the Passion and the Resurrection for the third time (20:17-19). This is a book of dramatic conflict between Jesus and the religious authorities, especially the Temple officials (21:12, 23). The parable of the vineyard workers (20:1-16) sets the stage between Jesus and those who believe they have special privilege with God. According to the parable, not only is God a "fair and just" employer, God is also a "generous" employer. The new community of God's people is called to rejoice about this, especially when our neighbors are the recipients of God's generosity.

The next three parables Jesus tells (21:28–22:14) are directly related to the religious authorities who are clearly begrudging of

God's generosity. These parables deal with Jesus' authority, which the chief priests and elders question, saying, "By what authority are you doing these things, and who gave you this authority?" (21:23). The three parables build on each other and present the history of salvation.

In the first parable (21:28-32), the tax collectors and prostitutes accept the message; in the second parable, the son is killed outside the vineyard (21:33-44); and in the third parable, the guest who does not have the wedding garment is thrown out of the banquet (22:1-14). Jesus does not spare his words, nor does he blush when it comes to the final showdown with his enemies. In his great discourse that denounces the scribes and Pharisees (Chapter 23), the judgment is ferocious and final.

Using the opening words "Woe to you!" Jesus levels seven attacks on his foes. The first woe is on leaders who use the keys of the kingdom to lock people out instead of aiding entry (23:13). The second woe concerns missionary activities that leave people more unfortunate than before encountering the missionaries (23:15). The third woe turns attention to the "small print," devised to circumvent the seriousness and responsibility of oath taking (23:16). The fourth woe points to the inability to distinguish what is important from the trivial (23:23). The fifth woe decries appearances that are deceptively clean but hearts that are unclean, greedy, and self-indulgent (23:25). The sixth woe admonishes against an external appearance of purity but internal corruption (23:27). The seventh woe focuses on false penance (23:29), which has played itself throughout history from "A to Z" (Abel to Zechariah, 23:35) and is reflected in the earlier parable of the vineyard (21:33-44). Unlike these foes, followers of Jesus are inconspicuous and quietly offer compassion to those who are hungry and hurting (25:31-46).

Epilogue: Matthew 26:2–28:20

Matthew's conclusion is in narrative form. At the beginning of this concluding book, Matthew gives a clear indication that Jesus' pas-

---

Look up these three parables. How would you describe the biblical images of obedience, faithfulness, respect or honor, and hospitality? Do you identify with any of the characters? If so, which ones and why?

Review the "woes" in Matthew 23. What are the woes? To whom are they addressed? How might they be paraphrased today? Are you involved in any practice that Jesus might condemn?

MATTHEW'S MESSAGE

sion occurs at the bidding of God. The Passion narrative unfolds with step-by-step deliberate movement toward the death. A woman anoints Jesus and prepares him for his burial (26:6-13); Judas agrees to betray Jesus (26:14-16); Jesus celebrates the Passover as the last earthly meal he eats with his disciples (26:17-30); Jesus foretells Peter's denial (26:31-35). In only a few paces we are in Gethsemane and the cup of death is inevitable (26:36-46). Jesus is betrayed by one of his own disciples, who later takes his own life (26:47-56; 27:3-10). Jesus is transferred from the religious court to the political court of Pilate (27:1-2). The crowd makes the verdict that Jesus is to be executed by crucifixion (27:15-23). After the mockery, Jesus is crucified on the place called Golgotha (27:32-37).

Like his birth, the death of Jesus is witnessed by Gentiles (here a centurion, 27:54) and by women. Jesus' mother Mary, Mary Magdalene, Mary the mother of two of Jesus' disciples, and many other women are among those who witness the death of Jesus (27:55-56). Matthew discloses that these women had been in the background of the narrative all along since they had "followed Jesus from Galilee and had provided for him" (27:55).

Even to the end Matthew continues to surprise us with the unexpected and anonymous followers of Jesus along the way. Just like Joseph who took care of Jesus of Nazareth when he was a helpless baby, another Joseph (of Arimathea) is among the surprising people whom God enlists to take care of the dead body of Jesus. Joseph's life is also invaded by God. Joseph gives up his own new tomb for Jesus (27:59-60).

The new life of resurrection that begins with the dawning day is witnessed by women and by Gentiles. "Mary Magdalene and the other Mary" (28:1) were the first to go to the tomb. These women and the guards at the tomb (most likely Roman guards and therefore Gentiles) witness the earthquake and that the stone

In Matthew 27:55, "provided for him" probably means that the women had at least offered financial support. What kinds of support do you think Jesus needed? Where might he have found it? When someone points to you and how you "provided for him," what would be said about you? Would this please you? Explain.

Look up Joseph of Arimathea in a Bible dictionary. What do you learn about him? What did he do for Jesus? What risks are you willing to take for Jesus Messiah?

has been rolled away. The guards, like Herod in the birth story, are filled with fear (28:4). They become like dead men. They report to the chief priests what has happened but are bribed to change their story (28:11-12).

Matthew ends with an account that explains the purpose of Matthew's church. Anyone who is not sure what the mission of the church is will find an answer in the Gospel's Great Commission (28:16-20), which sets the agenda for the church.

The church is called to live out a life like the life of Jesus. The church is to go and make disciples as Jesus did. But unlike Jesus, the church has a mission to all nations. Just as Jesus was baptized, the church is commissioned to baptize new disciples and to teach the new Torah that Jesus has given us. Reflecting the words of *Emmanuel*, which means "God is with us," the parting words of Jesus Messiah echo God's presence with us now, through all the millennia that God would give, and beyond, "to the end of the age."

> **The parting words of Jesus Messiah echo God's presence with us now, through all the millennia, and beyond, "to the end of the age."**

The story starts and ends, for some, with fear. What are some of the consequences of those fears? What do you do when you are afraid? when you are afraid because of faith obligations?

Read the Great Commission (Matthew 28:16-20). What are the disciples' "marching orders"? Do you consider these words your own commission? Explain. If so, how do you live out that commission?

Do you feel and believe that God is present with you "through all the millennia"? Explain. Take time in prayer to dedicate or rededicate your life to Jesus Messiah and to accept or accept anew your own commission to discipleship.

MATTHEW'S MESSAGE

MATTHEW DIAGNOSES THE HUMAN CONDITION

Since the Gospel of Matthew is two millennia older than we are, some might think that all this happened a long time ago and therefore is outdated, old-fashioned, and obsolete. Some of us might argue that Matthew's world was so different from our world that there is no way Matthew could have anything to say about the third millennium's context, ranging from holocausts and ethnic cleansings to outer space technology.

Matthew wrote his Gospel long before the invention of bicycles, cars, and airplanes. Would Matthew therefore be understood only in the parts of the world where walking is still the major mode of transport?

Matthew wrote his Gospel long before Christopher Columbus stumbled into the Americas and long before David Livingstone went to Africa. Would Matthew understand about pilgrims seeking a better world or about the annihilation of native peoples or about slavery and colonialism?

Matthew wrote his Gospel long before the discovery of penicillin, polio vaccinations, and quinine. When we encounter the good news for those who are sick or demon possessed in the Gospel of Matthew, we might have ideas that are very different from Matthew's ideas of disease and healing. Would Matthew understand the world of modern science and medicine?

Our world is so different from Matthew's world! If we take our situation seriously, can Matthew's Gospel possibly be relevant to our human condition in the third millennium? Matthew's Gospel revolves around community, and the theme of relationships is a recurring theme; how are Christians to relate to others, and how

From your current knowledge about Matthew's Gospel and world, what parallels do you see? What differences?

are Christians to relate to God? For Matthew, the good news of God's saving presence is in the life, ministry, and passion of Jesus Messiah. It comes as a big surprise that Matthew's Gospel is the perfect Gospel for the new millennium. Because Matthew's Gospel is about God's saving presence amidst changes and crises, endings and beginnings in an increasingly pluralistic society, Matthew speaks precisely to our situation. Perhaps it is because Matthew's situation was very much like our situation.

Matthew's Gospel is about God's saving presence amidst changes and crises, endings and beginnings in an increasingly pluralistic society.

A Broken World

For Matthew, the core of being human is authentic, faithful relationships. Human beings were created for relationships with each other and with God. Therefore our deepest and most basic human need is authentic, enduring, and faithful relationship with each other and with God. Matthew would be unbending on the importance of relationship regardless of our modern concept of independence and individualistic lifestyle. Matthew would be especially concerned with relationships between people of the world.

At the 1997 Pre-Institute Third World Consultation of the Oxford Institute, Methodist scholars from Africa, Asia, and South America gave a report on the state of the world. Their grim findings: "Market forces are concentrating wealth in the hands of a few. The gross product of the world has grown three times in the past 30 years, yet 80 percent of that product is consumed by only 20 percent of the world population. The 20 percent at the bottom have only 1.4 percent of the gross product. The 359 largest personal fortunes are equal to the total income of 2 billion of the world's people. Similar statistics reveal the same pattern for energy consumption, educational opportunities and health care expenditures" (*Sharing our Time Together*, Pre-Institute Third World Consultation, Oxford Institute, 1997).

How do you think Christians should relate to God and to each other?

What, for you, is the core of being human? How does your understanding of community mesh with your concept of individuality?

What is the ratio in your congregation between those who have much and those who have little?

At the World Methodist Conference in Brazil, Leonard Sweet's shocking address revealed that 27,000 species go extinct each year; 2 billion people live in countries with an average per capita income of $400; 40 percent of the world's population lives in poverty and suffers from malnutrition. The other side of the coin is just as shocking with people in superpower countries spending $15 billion per year on losing weight and an extra $22 billion on beauty aids. Furthermore, in 1992 the leading American basketball player earned $20 million to promote Nike shoes, which was more than the entire annual payroll of all the Indonesian factories that make the shoes!

More than ever before in human history, the rift between the haves and the have nots is unsurpassed in terms of quality of life as well as greed. Our world is becoming more and more divided along economic lines.

Putting a Human Face on Power

Matthew addresses our broken relationships as a manifestation of disobedience—the compulsion for control and power and an inability to yield our pride and be vulnerable. Herod is a prime example of an unsound human core that is rife with broken relationships. Although Herod was nearly sixty years old when Jesus was born, we see the birth of a baby filling him with fright (Matthew 2:1-3). Herod was so insecure that his need to control and his desire to amass more personal power blinded him to his own mortality. In fact, three years after Jesus' birth, Herod was dead (2:19).

Herod's compulsion for control obsessed him and drove him first to fear (2:3), then to lie (2:8), and finally to explode into a mad fury that killed "all the children in and around Bethlehem who were two years old or under" (2:16).

Herod's blind lust for power at the price of lives is similar to that of the pharaohs (Exodus 1:15-22), the Hitlers, and the Pol Pots of our world.

Called to Be Different

The disciples of Jesus are called to be different from Herod. When

What does the Gospel tell you about the stewardship of resources?

Read Matthew 2:1-19. What sort of portrait do you see of Herod? What seems to motivate him? Where is the hand of God in these events?

Read Matthew 19:13-15 and 18:1-5. The baby Jesus escaped death though many other children died. What effect might this have had on Jesus' ministry to children? What does Jesus teach us about children in these passages?

the disciples exercised their power and sternly refused the children access to Jesus, Jesus immediately made room for children, inviting them to him and teaching his disciples to always give preference to children (Matthew 19:13-15). Furthermore, children are not only welcome in the Jesus community; children model the life of the believer in their being constantly at risk (18:1-5).

Matthew's Gospel invites us to learn the art of building and staying in healthy, thriving relationships

Matthew discloses our basic lack of courage to take a risk in a new relationship and a tendency to be comfortable in what we have known in the past regardless of our lack of success in the past. Perhaps we are afraid of being manipulated or "used" because of what we have or who we are. Perhaps due to our past experiences, we find it difficult to be vulnerable in relationships. Perhaps the scar of painful memories or experience of betrayal, deception, or abuse by those we have trusted in the past make it difficult to risk other relationships. We are therefore more familiar with broken relationships than with safe, healthy, and thriving relationships (see 18:23-35; 21:28-32, 33-44).

With a depth in understanding the human condition, Matthew's Gospel invites us to learn the art of building and staying in healthy, thriving relationships by introducing us to people who model risk-taking; radical trust in their relationship with God; and authentic, compassionate relationships with others.

A Multicultural World

The Gospel of Matthew is the perfect gospel for the new millennium. Matthew has a pluralistic and multicultural diversity. Like our own world, Matthew's world is rich with surprising, unexpected, and interesting people. Matthew's vision extends the circle of discipleship and finds followers of Jesus in people from every stratum of society and in all kinds of situations. Matthew's Gospel prepares us to meet the world and encourages us to expect surprises in meeting disci-

How does your faith empower you to be a risk and to take risks?

Review these passages (18:23-35; 21:28-32, 33-44). What do they teach about the human condition, God's will, and God's grace?

From your current knowledge of the disciples, how do you think they are like and unlike you?

ples who are so like and so unlike ourselves. In the Gospel of Matthew, we meet ordinary people who dare to take risks for God, who trust in radical ways, and who show authentic compassion for others.

In Matthew's Gospel, we meet men, women, and children, peoples from different ethnic, social, and economic backgrounds. Although in Matthew, Jesus' ministry is limited to the house of Israel, Matthew nevertheless crosses ethnic boundaries and introduces us to both Jews and Gentiles: a Roman soldier and a Canaanite woman; a Cyrenean farmer and wise men from the East. Matthew also crosses social/economic boundaries and introduces us to the haves and the have nots, the rich and the poor, the powerful and the disenfranchised. We meet a refugee family on the run from a wicked king (2:19-23), a princess who dances and asks for a prophet's head as reward (14:1-12), and a governor's wife who dreams disturbing dreams and warns her husband (27:15-19).

In the Gospel of Matthew, the sick, the blind, and those who are demon-possessed seek out Jesus, follow Jesus, and are healed and restored. (See, for example, 8:1-17, 28-33; 9:27-29.) Matthew points out religious leaders and political leaders for us and allows us to overhear them challenge Jesus (9:10-13; 12:1-8). The people we meet in Matthew work in a variety of jobs. Some are self-employed (4:18), and others work for the government (8:5).

The Gospel of Matthew is a gospel where each one in the new millennium community can find people that resemble their kinfolk and neighbors! The Gospel of Matthew is a gospel for our world today.

Introducing Joseph

One of my favorite people in the Gospel of Matthew is Joseph. Joseph plays quite a central role at the beginning of Matthew's Gospel. Joseph then falls into the background of the narrative as Jesus occupies the center stage. Joseph is not to be confused as Jesus' father. Jesus is the Son of God. In their hometown of Nazareth, Jesus is later referred to as merely "the car-

Look up 2:19-23; 14:1-12; 27:15-19. Who are the main characters? How do their actions, inactions, and attitudes shape how Jesus' life unfolds? How might his life and ministry have been different if a different decision had been made?

Look up 9:10-13 and 12:1-8 How is Jesus confronted by these leaders? What does he do? What are the consequences?

penter's son" without Joseph being named (13:55). Nevertheless, although there is no place that designates Joseph as a disciple or follower of Jesus, Joseph is a role model par excellence of Christian discipleship, especially for us in the third millennium.

We are told that Joseph is a thinker who ponders, struggles, and takes time to arrive at a solution for a problem when it involves another person. How very unlike the third millennium's culture of instant solutions!

When it comes to decisions about relationships with others, Joseph does not expect a quick, instant solution. Take, for instance, Joseph's certain disappointment when he learned of Mary's unexpected pregnancy (1:18-19). Since he knew from his relationship with Mary that he was not the father of his fiancée's child, we would expect Joseph to have swiftly and quickly decided to divorce Mary. But Joseph shows us a different way of dealing with those who have disap-

> **Joseph is a thinker who ponders, struggles, and takes time to arrive at a solution. How very unlike the third millennium's culture of instant solutions!**

pointed us (1:24). We see Joseph taking time to think and struggle with disappointment. We see Joseph's decision as one that is not based on himself, but as one that considers Mary. Being a righteous man and keeping with the Law, Joseph is a compassionate man who tries to think of a way to spare Mary public trial and humiliation. Without seeking redress and revenge for the disappointment Mary has caused him, Joseph resolves in his heart to quietly divorce Mary.

A Prophetic Dream

Then comes the dream (1:20-21). Joseph is asked to reverse his decision and yield his life to God's plan. In a dream, Joseph is given a revelation as well as special information about the situation he thought was a problem or a misfortune. It turns out that Mary's pregnancy is part of God's work of salvation. Mary's pregnancy is not a random event but instead is a designed fulfillment of prophecy. Mary, then, has been

Look up Joseph in a Bible dictionary. What do we know about him?

Read Matthew 1:18-25. How do Mary and Joseph enter into God's plan? How do you think they felt?

MATTHEW'S MESSAGE

faithful to Joseph. Mary has also been obedient to God.

Joseph is to play a major role as the link between the child and David's royal bloodline. He is to take the pregnant Mary for his wife and take the responsibility of naming Mary's child when he is born. He is to name the child "Jesus," because "he will save his people from their sins." The child is Emmanuel, a sign of God's presence with God's people (1:21-23; Isaiah 7:10-14).

Waking up from such a disturbing dream, what will Joseph do? If he obeys, he must reverse his very fair decision to divorce Mary quietly. If he obeys, he will be showing trust toward Mary as a faithful betrothed. If Joseph obeys, he will be yielding the rest of his life into a relationship with a son whose role as Savior might cost him his life. God was asking Joseph to take on a long-term commitment. Surely if Joseph had reservations about the dream and had disobeyed, we would understand. Joseph chooses to obey! He takes Mary as his wife and cares for her until she bears a son. It is Joseph who names the newborn baby Jesus. Obedience in swift action marks Joseph as a disciple. God can depend on Joseph.

Joseph's obedience to God changed his life completely. Soon after Jesus' birth and naming, Joseph received yet another dream: Herod the king was a threat to Jesus; Joseph must take Jesus and his mother and flee to Egypt.

The Refugee Family

It is amazing that a king would be so greatly threatened by a tiny, helpless baby. Joseph awoke from the dream; and as was his nature, he obeyed and acted immediately. In the cover of night, Joseph made a speedy exit from his familiar native land into the unknown land of Egypt. This displacement and exile placed the Son of God within the prophecy of Hosea that "out of Egypt I called my son" (Hosea 11:1). Furthermore, as a child refugee, Jesus Messiah reenacted the historical experience of his people and could now represent them. The history of refugees and exile reminds the Holy Family that even in exile God's providence is at work. Even in exile, *Emmanuel*, "God is with us." Therefore no

If you thought God was asking you something so radical (as Joseph was), how might you respond? Why?

Read Matthew 2:19-23. How might this exile experience have affected Jesus' ministry? Give reasons for your response.

refugee or exile is outside divine concern and care. Jesus as a refugee affirms that, once and for all.

Through his obedience, Joseph became the agent God used to fulfill two major prophecies. Through Joseph's obedience, Jesus Messiah began his ministry solidly rooted in David's ancestry. With the firsthand experience of Egypt, exile, and return, Joseph was a disciple par excellence.

So Like Us

The people we meet in the Gospel of Matthew are like us; they are ordinary people whom Jesus Messiah calls into a radical and obedient life of discipleship. Although in our admiration we may put these people on a pedestal, they were not extraordinary. They were people like us with hopes and struggles, flaws in character, and strengths, doubts, and fears. When we encounter some of them, they are so human, they embarrass us! Perhaps that is why we can easily identify with them although they are two millennia older than we are. Who are they? Parents who, like all parents, want the best for their children (7:11); leaders in the church who forget they are called for servant leadership and not worldly greatness (20:26-27); disciples who are supposed to be role models but are so hot tempered they get nicknamed "sons of Thunder" (Mark 3:17); followers of Jesus who not only miss the point about the kingdom of heaven but also have terrible timing, ask the wrong question, and make the wrong requests.

Meet James, John, and Family

Take, for instance, the mother of James and John. When we meet her, she has just asked an ill-timed question that reveals her terrible misunderstanding about the kingdom of God (Matthew 20:20-28). These brothers, James and John, had previously been fishermen when Jesus saw them in their family boat with their father, mending their nets. When Jesus called the brothers to follow him, they had immediately abandoned both their boat and their father and followed Jesus (4:18-22).

Review 7:11 and 20:26-27. What do they teach us about the human condition? About your condition?

Read Matthew 20:20-28. What was the mother asking? What would be the consequences if the request were granted? Why do you think the other disciples were angry?

It is not clear what happened at the Zebedee home that night, but we later learn that James and John's mother was named Mary and was one of the women who had "followed Jesus from Galilee and had provided for him" (27:55-56). In Mark, we learn that Jesus had nicknamed these two brothers *Boanerges,* which means Sons of Thunder (Mark 3:17).

We can only guess about their quick temper and rash action, especially when they suggested annihilating a Samaritan village with fire (Luke 9:51-56)! Nevertheless, Jesus seemed to have a special place for these two brothers; and they accompanied Jesus in the prominent events of the Transfiguration (Matthew 17:1) and in Gethsemane (26:37).

Perhaps because of this close association, their mother wanted to be assured of their close association in heaven (20:20-28). In Mark, the disciples themselves, and not their mother, requested the special places of greatness in his kingdom (Mark 10:35-40). Many scholars think Mark's account is probably accurate because Jesus addresses his answer to James and John and not to their mother (Matthew 20:22).

Whatever the case is, Matthew's account of the incident certainly buffers our indignation with the two brothers and preserves their integrity. Nevertheless, these disciples and their mother were not so different from us. Although they were seeking status and honor in the kingdom of heaven, they were using the world's values for the kingdom. The brothers were asking for something that was beyond their grasp. Just as their story appears in Matthew 20:20, they too lack twenty-twenty vision! No wonder the story of the two brothers is immediately followed by the story of the healing of two blind men (20:29-34). Jesus' eyes are always open to the fragile human condition. Those whose lives are touched "regain their sight and follow him."

How do you "provide for Jesus' ministry"?

Read Matthew 20:29-34. How has your faith in Jesus opened your eyes to others? Take a moment in prayer to dedicate or rededicate your life to Christ.

MATTHEW TELLS US ABOUT JESUS CHRIST

Matthew uses different titles and names for Jesus in order to give us large amounts of information about Jesus in a very concise way. For Matthew, titles and names can change the way we think about someone. Titles can change a perspective we might have about a person. For instance, Jane Doe can be transformed into someone distinguished by a title that designates her as Princess Jane Doe. Titles can also be helpful ways of giving information about persons. Therefore, one person can have different titles depending on the circumstances, the context, the information that needs to be given or the impression that needs to be made. For example in a PTA meeting, it would make more sense to address Dr. Doe as John or as Jane's father. In a family reunion, a pastor can be a daughter, a granddaughter, a niece, and a cousin. In a football match, a student who is someone's brother or son becomes to the spectators and fans simply a position in a game, such as a quarterback.

Likewise, in the Gospel of Matthew Jesus has many titles. Among them, Jesus is called Son of David (12:23), Lord (15:25), Teacher or Rabbi (19:16), and the Son of God (27:54). By using these titles, Matthew gives us large amounts of information about the identity of Jesus and his relationship to those who address him.

The Function of Titles

Titles are supposed to function in a certain way. In order to function correctly, there is an assumption that the reader knows the historical or cultural association of the title. Otherwise the title becomes

What do titles imply to you? Does your opinion or attitude change toward someone if you discover that he or she has a title? doesn't have the title you thought he or she had?

meaningless or becomes simply another name. For instance, if we were introduced to someone as Kabaka Mwanga and we were not familiar with the Baganda people of Uganda, we might think the man's personal name was Kabaka and his surname was Mwanga. How far from the truth that would be! For the Baganda people, *Kabaka* is synonymous with *king,* and we would have met King Mwanga. But if we did not know any better and the man told us he was a refugee or was homeless, we might assume he was one of the millions of displaced people in the world. We would not realize he was giving us information of a political situation that forces a king into exile. In fact we could spend the whole day with the Kabaka and miss the historical, cultural, and political significance of what he might say or what those around him say.

This is also true for Matthew's use of the title *Messiah* or the *Christ* (1:1; 16:16). Many of us are so used to hearing "Jesus Christ" we might think that Christ is Jesus' surname. We shall study closely the title *Christ* and what it means, who uses it, and its implications. Understanding the significance of a title can be helpful in processing and interpreting information and situations.

The Community Behind the Person

Titles also point to a community behind the person. An individual cannot give himself or herself a title. A community gives an individual a title. Titles are the property of a community and often a title is bigger than the individual who bears it. Therefore there is significantly more at stake when a title is used rather than the individual's name. For example a report saying "a man has been shot" or "John has been shot," although accurate, do not have the same impact as the same report saying "the Pope has been shot." As soon as a title is used, there is an appeal to a particular community and its agenda. In our modern world, the titles of "reverend" or "rabbi" or "imam" immediately point to religious community. The titles of "doctor" and "professor" point to academic communities. Titles given by families tell us about the relationship between the kin of "uncle," "auntie," "mum," or "dad." Titles of "queen," "sir," and "senator" tell us of political and imperial communities and indicate the political climate of accounts involving these persons.

All of this is to say that titles are powerful clues to the relation-

What do titles suggest about the community in which they "reside"? How do titles influence the community?

ships in a community. Titles give clues about the community behind the individual; the historical, cultural, or political circumstances of the account; and the role of the individual.

In Matthew's Gospel, Jesus' hometown of Nazareth fails to recognize who he is because they describe him with inadequate titles. The town of Nazareth sees Jesus as merely "the carpenter's son" and "Mary's son," and "the brother of James and Joseph and Simon and Judas" (13:55). Jesus challenges these titles when his mother and brothers arrive to see him by calling his disciples his true family. For Jesus, "whoever does the will of my Father in heaven is my brother and sister and mother" (12:50).

The Importance of Naming

Personal names function in similar ways to titles. Many African societies, for instance, give a child a name that functions as a claim, or a title, about him or her. Among the Meru of East Africa, a child is always named after a relative, depending on gender and position in birth. The child's *ntagu* or namesake gives a name that describes his or her life and the hope for the child. For instance, a grandmother who was known for her beauty as a young woman would name her namesake-granddaughter "Nkatha"; and an uncle who is widely traveled or is known to be a good walker will name his nephew, "Mwiti." Among the Meru people, just by knowing someone's name, it is easy to know what the history of the person's family is and what hopes have been placed on the individual.

Naming is an important biblical activity. The first instance we see is in Genesis 1 with God creating the universe. Each created element receives its designation from God. We read that "God called the light Day, and the darkness he called Night" (Genesis 1:5). Then God created the first human and gave that person the task of naming all the other living creatures.

We read, among other stories, that Jacob wrestled with "an angel." Part of the contest involved the request by Jacob to know his

Look up Matthew 13:55 for the context of this remark about Jesus. What happens when we label someone so that he or she can be dismissed as "just the carpenter's son"?

What naming stories do you remember in the Bible? Locate them in the Scriptures if you can. What do those stories signify in their own context? to you? Do you know what your own name means? Is that significant for you? Why?

adversary's name; but instead he was given a new name, "Israel," as "one who strives with God" (Genesis 32:22-32). Some prophets named their children to reflect the condition of the general populace (see, for example, Hosea 1:2-8). One significant point of all these incidences is that, in naming, the one who designates or gives the name has an intimate knowledge of the one named. This intimacy includes a depth of relationship that goes beyond mere acquaintanceship or even kinship. It implies a connection, a responsibility, a relationship bound by more than just familiarity. Sometimes the name is designation by a human in response to a transformational encounter with the divine; sometimes the divine announces to the human subject what a place or child is to be named.

There have been times in our history when an individual's personal name has come to be a

> **One significant point of all these incidences is that, in naming, the one who designates or gives the name has an intimate knowledge of the one named.**

title. An individual might embody certain qualities or achievements so that the personal name gradually becomes more of a title than a name. In twentieth-century history, people like Kwame Nkurumah, Mahatma Gandhi, Martin Luther King Jr., Malcolm X, and Mother Teresa have been so greatly associated with a cause that their entire names are more like titles. (This works with villains as well. We know that describing someone as a Hitler conveys an enormous import.)

Sorting Out the Cast of Characters

In the Gospel of Matthew, the name of Herod functions in this way. No wonder it can get rather confusing when working with the Herods! It can help to keep in mind that Herod is a family name, and in Matthew's Gospel we meet four different Herods.

Who "knows your name" so well that he or she has intimate knowledge of you? What responsibility does that knowledge carry? Who do you know so intimately? What responsibility does that knowledge impart to you?

Look up *Herod* in a Bible dictionary to sort out which Herod is which. What do you learn about the Herods who appear in Jesus' story?

MATTHEW'S MESSAGE

King Herod the Great whom we meet when Jesus is born (2:1, 16) dies during Jesus' childhood (2:19). Although Matthew does not give us the details, at Herod's death, the kingdom was divided among his three sons who were half-brothers: Herod Archelaus, Herod Philip, and Herod Antipas.

Matthew tells us that Joseph decided not to return to Judea because Archelaus ruled there (2:22). Archelaus ruled for only a short time. He was a brutal king, and his territory became a Roman province. Hence when Jesus was tried in Jerusalem, he appeared before a Roman governor and not before a Herod.

The other half-brother, Herod Philip, rebuilt the town of Caesarea Philippi (16:13). (He is not the same Philip who was married to Herodias, who later married Herod Antipas.) Herod Antipas ruled Galilee; and since Galilee was the area of ministry for John the Baptist and for Jesus, Antipas figures in the Gospels quite often. Antipas was the one who murdered John the Baptist. He was in a scandalous affair and later a marriage to Herodias, a very close and married relative, which John the Baptist had challenged (14:3). Antipas rewarded the dance of Salome, Herodias's daughter, with the head of John the Baptist on a platter (14:5-11).

But Who Do You Say That I Am?

One of the most dramatic scenes in the Gospel of Matthew occurs between Jesus and his disciple Peter in the district of Caesarea Philippi, a Roman city (16:13-20). In this scene, Jesus asks Peter two consecutive questions; both questions are about the identity of Jesus. The first question is "Who do people say that the Son of Man is?" (16:13).

According to Peter, there are four main understandings of who Jesus is. There is a group who says Jesus is John the Baptist, another group who says Jesus is the prophet Elijah, another who says Jesus is Jeremiah, and another who says Jesus is one of the prophets (16:14). Jesus places Peter on his own personal level by then asking him: "But who do you say that I am?" (16:15). Peter's reply that "you are the Messiah, the Son of the living God" (16:16) is Matthew's testimony. The entire Gospel of Matthew is a testimony that Jesus is Messiah, Son of the living God.

Review Matthew 16:13-20, and look up that passage in a Bible commentary for a more complete explanation. What is the significance of each of these other characters who Jesus is thought to be? Why, when Peter got the identity right, did Jesus ask the disciples not to tell anyone?

Titles for Jesus

The Gospel of Matthew gives us a great amount of information about Jesus by using a variety of titles for Jesus. The name *Jesus* itself carries the meaning of Jesus' life and ministry. *Jesus* means "he will save his people from their sins" (1:21), which he does. Through time, the name *Jesus* has come to function more like a title than a personal name. In some parts of our world, although children are named Moses and Elijah and Mary, the name *Jesus* is set apart as too reverent to use. It is a name that carries tremendous spiritual and religious meaning.

Yet surprisingly enough, in other parts of our world people feel quite comfortable naming their children Jesus. In addition to Jesus,

Christ is a title in Greek. It means "anointed one." It is a translation of the Hebrew Messiah. Christ and Messiah are the same word in different languages.

Matthew uses the titles of Christ, Messiah, Son of David, Lord, Son of Man, Son of God, and King of the Jews. In addition to these titles, Matthew treats Jesus in ways that remind us of other titles. Matthew treats Jesus as The Servant of Yahweh, Wisdom, and Emmanuel.

The Christ, the Messiah, the Anointed One

The title *Christ* is so familiar that we often assume it is Jesus' surname. When we do that, we miss the radical implications of the title "Christ." *Christ* is a title in Greek. It means "anointed one." It is a translation of the Hebrew *Messiah. Christ* and *Messiah* are the same word in different languages.

In the Old Testament the only people who were anointed by

What does *Jesus* mean? How have you experienced Jesus "living up to his name"?

What other names or attributions, from any source, have you heard for Jesus? Locate them in the Bible if you can. What name or characteristic carries the most force or appeal for you? Why?

What does *Christ* or *Messiah* mean? Look up *anointing* in a Bible dictionary. Who is anointed and why? What is the significance of anointing in the biblical context? When is anointing done today, and what does it mean?

God were high priests and kings. Occasionally prophets could also be anointed. In Israel's tradition, the Messiah was prophesied as the Coming One who was foretold by the prophets and awaited by Israel. The Messiah was expected to be a kingly figure who would stand in the royal line of David and bring the history of Israel to its culmination. Matthew begins his Gospel by identifying Jesus as Messiah (1:1) because, from the onset, Matthew's testimony is that Jesus is the Messiah. The title of Jesus as Messiah occurs in three episodes in the Gospel where the question of Jesus' identity comes to the forefront (11:2-3;16:16; 26:63-64).

One's identity was tied to his family, and Jesus is reckoned as Joseph's son, "descended from the house and family of David" (Luke 2:4). King David, though having his own misdeeds chronicled and criticized, was regarded as the paradigm, or model, of the good

> **Through the twisted and tortuous turns of Israel's history, the hope went before the people that a king from the house of David would return to rule in peace with justice.**

and faithful king. Through the twisted and tortuous turns of Israel's history, the hope went before the people that a king from the house of David would return to rule in peace with justice. That Jesus was known to be of the family of David made it possible to imagine that he might be the promised Messiah.

The Son of David

Matthew also calls Jesus "son of David" (Matthew 9:27; 12:23; 15:22; 20:30; 21:9). In the account of Jesus' triumphant entry into Jerusalem, the title of Jesus as Son of David can be most clearly understood (20:29-34). As Jesus and a large crowd leave Jericho heading to Jerusalem, two blind men sitting by the road begin to cry out for mercy from Jesus, saying, "Lord, have mercy on us, Son of David!" (20:30). The blind men acknowledge Jesus' royal lineage, his political rank, and his messianic standing. Although the crowd warns these two blind men

---

Look up *David* in a Bible dictionary. Why was his kingship so significant for Israel? What are the prophecies about the future king from the line of David?

Look up these passages that refer to Jesus as the Son of David. What is their context? Why does this name for Jesus seem so powerful?

---

to be silent, they cry all the more. When Jesus finally stops and asks them, "What do you want me to do for you?" they reply, "Lord, let our eyes be opened" (20:32-33). Jesus is moved by compassion; he touches their eyes; and immediately their sight is restored. Unlike the earlier blind men who, when healed, went away to spread the good news (9:27-31), these two blind men become followers and continue with Jesus into Jerusalem (20:34).

When Jesus enters Jerusalem—it is the final leg of his ministry—he enters as a humble king (21:5). He comes from the house of David, and the entire history of Israel culminates in him. Therefore the scene has political overtones that fulfill the prophet's words: "Tell the daughter of Zion, / Look, your king is coming to you, / humble, and mounted on a donkey" (21:5). He is the king of his people in the sense that he suffers on their behalf.

Jesus, the Son of God

Jesus is the Son of God. Although Jesus is born of the virgin Mary and adopted by Joseph, the origin of Jesus is God, and he is God's Beloved. In two transformational events, we see Jesus identified as the Beloved Son of God. The first is his baptism (3:13-17); the second, the Transfiguration (17:1-13). In both instances, a voice from heaven announces Jesus as the beloved Son in whom God is pleased. In the Transfiguration, the voice of God goes beyond announcement to commandment and admonishes the hearers to listen.

Each proclamation of Jesus' sonship carries the weight of authority, but an authority that is grounded in love. This is the *beloved* Son. He has come to demonstrate, firsthand and close up, just what the love of God is. That love is grace-filled and transformational, powerful and

Review the story of Jesus' baptism (Matthew 3:13-16). What happens? Whose voice is heard? Who hears it? What does it mean? Do you remember your own baptism or the baptism of someone special to you? Did you have the sense of the divine word being spoken about God's love toward you or to the person being baptized? How would you describe that experience and its effect on you?

Read the story of the Transfiguration (Matthew 17:1-13). Who are the key witnesses in the story? Who appears before them and what is their significance? Have you ever had the sense of being in the immediate presence of God's beloved Son? If so, how did it feel? What lasting effect, if any, did it have?

dynamic; it leads to a life of risk and of doing justice.

Jesus' ministry was inaugurated by the announcement of his sonship at his baptism.

The story of the baptism is crucial to the portrait of Jesus as Son of God. Jesus does not submit to baptism by John because he has need to repent of sin or because he needs to be become a disciple of John. On the contrary, Jesus submits to baptism because it is the will of God that he and John should "fulfill all righteousness."

In brief, Jesus submits to baptism by John according to Matthew because God wills it; and Jesus renders to God perfect obedience. For Matthew, righteousness means conduct that is in agreement with God's will and well pleasing to God. Righteousness is not a step toward the kingdom of heaven. Righteousness is the blood and sap of the kingdom

> **Jesus is uniquely the Son of God in a way that cannot be ascribed to another human being.**

of heaven (5:6, 10; 6:20). The only way to please God is to be righteous.

Although the disciples enter into fellowship with God and hence become "sons of God," only Jesus alone is the "son of God." Jesus is therefore uniquely the Son of God in a way that cannot be ascribed to another human being. In consequence of the unique relationship that exists between Jesus the Son and God his Father, the Father entrusts the Son with divine authority.

Through Jesus, Son of God, God has drawn near with his present and future rule to dwell to the end of time with his people, the church. God is therefore uniquely present and at work in Jesus. By becoming Jesus' disciple, one becomes a child of God, lives in the sphere of his end-time rule, and engages in mission to the end that all people may find God in Jesus and become Jesus' disciples.

What is *righteousness*? Using a concordance, see how many times the term *righteous* or *righteousness* is mentioned, and look up a few of the passages. Are you righteous, in the best sense of the term? Is that possible for humans other than Jesus?

How do you understand your own relationship to Jesus and to God? Do you see yourself as a child of God in the way that Jesus is the Son of God? Do you see yourself as a beloved child of God? Explain.

Those disciples are also beloved in the kingdom of heaven.

In the dramatic scene between Jesus and his disciple Peter in the district of Caesarea Philippi, a Roman city (16:13-20), Jesus asked Peter two questions. Both questions were about the identity of Jesus. The first question, "Who do people say that the Son of Man is?" (16:13) was followed quickly with the question on a personal level of "But who do you say that I am?" (16:15). The entire Gospel of Matthew is a testimony to both of these questions so that the reader might know and come to believe.

Who do you think Jesus is? What titles or attributions do you give to Jesus? How do those identifiers help you understand your relationship with Jesus?

God wants you to have a relationship through Jesus Christ. Take a moment in prayer to commit or recommit your life and work to Jesus the Christ, and ask for his guidance to do so.

MATTHEW CLARIFIES OUR VISION

When we look at the overwhelming complexity of the world today, we are quite amazed that a first-century evangelist like Matthew not only understands our times so clearly but is a capable guide for us as we negotiate our entry into the third millennium. In spirit, Matthew is very much alive today and continues to actively comment on our times.

Every sermon that is preached from Matthew's Gospel is Matthew speaking, no matter how haltingly, through an interpreter for our times. Every Bible study on Matthew is a way of taking time to listen to Matthew speak. Every play and painting and hymn that has been inspired by Matthew is Matthew speaking.

Matthew is very much alive and relevant today.

As we listen to Matthew, we are amazed that Matthew is so appropriate for our times. Perhaps Matthew's Gospel resonates with us so deeply because the milieu of first-century Palestine resembles our own turbulent times. Our times are very similar to Matthew's because we are experiencing many of the changes that took place in first-century Palestine in terms of religious identity, culture, and relationships with peoples from whom we were previously separated. Matthew's church was experiencing the same questions and growing pains that we are now laboring through.

When you hear hymns, poems, or stories that are based on a portion of Matthew, does that seem to you as if Matthew is speaking to you? What sense of connection do you feel to the Scriptures?

Matthew's world faced the destruction of the Temple in Jerusalem and the occupation of that city by Rome. What contemporary parallels can you think of for our culture and our religious spheres?

Just like us, Matthew faced two main issues: the collapse of traditional paradigms and the practice of a Christian faith that included very different peoples and cultures and histories. So Matthew seems to know us and understand us; and he encourages us in our testimony for Jesus in the third millennium.

Affirming Differences

First and foremost, Matthew affirms us in our differences. According to Matthew, "many will come from east and west and will eat with Abraham and Isaac and Jacob in the kingdom of heaven" (8:11). Matthew is neither colorblind nor culture blind! In fact, Matthew celebrates the East and West about us. Therefore who we are matters to Matthew. Matthew seems to understand that who we are by nation, race, language, or social location is a gift we bring into the community of believers.

One thinker has argued that each of our social positions makes certain knowledge impossible to access. The kind of knowledge she talks about is not information that can be acquired by reading a book or magazine or downloading a program. Rather this knowledge comes only in being in relationships to those who are very different from us. Unfortunately for us, we are more familiar with differences being a source of disaster rather than strength.

Human history shows that when we have encountered people who are different from us, we have engaged in power struggles loaded with strategies of silencing others or ridiculing others or simply killing off people. Hence our history is often about conquering and domination and slavery and imperialism and colonialism and exploitation and racism and tribalism and sexism and bloodshed and genocide and holocausts and ethnic cleansings. Our track

Who was Matthew referring to, do you think, in Matthew 8:11? What does it mean that Matthew is neither colorblind nor culture blind?

How does our social position influence the information we can access and the information we consider to be more authoritative? Is Scripture just one possible source, or a definitive source for our world? for you? Explain.

What power struggles do you recall in Matthew's Gospel? What in your nation's history is "about conquering and ethnic cleansings"? How does that affect your view of and hope for the future?

MATTHEW'S MESSAGE

record in relationships with people who are different is so bad that it is difficult to be realistic and optimistic about our future.

No wonder, then, that every day we are bombarded with the same story after story about how impossible it is for different people to gather in the same place without somebody silencing somebody else in the myriad ways people have of silencing people including, disempowering and killing one another.

Every day CNN and the BBC carry stories of people gunning down each other because they are Roman Catholic in Protestant zones, or Protestants in Roman Catholic zones, or Hutus in Tutsi homelands, or vice versa. Every day newspapers are full of stories of policies voted in and laws made to keep some people living the same old ghetto lives because of the color of their skin. We get documentaries and special coverage of people who have chopped up each other with the blessings of their churches.

One part of the Rwanda story that terrifies us is that a country can turn into a graveyard within weeks. Within one hundred days, a million people were chopped up like firewood with machetes. Most of the victims were hacked to death by people they had known all their lives. Even more tragic is that ninety percent of the people of Rwanda are baptized and claim to be confessing Christians. Yet something sinister took over and snapped the theological foundations into kindling; nobody could subdue the madness.

In "The Angels Have Left Us" a sixteen-year-old girl named Josephine survived the genocide and gave international reporters a tour of her dead village. She took them to the church in which she was baptized and whispered, "We will never come back to this church. It is a graveyard. The angels have left us." In Rwanda, a priest was found guilty of assisting in the ethnic slaughter of a few years ago.

Emmanuel—God With Us

Matthew's Gospel gives testimony to God who comes to salvage our

How does the world news reflect the impact of the gospel? Is globalization another form of imperialism? Explain.

What might make neighbors, even Christian neighbors, turn against each other?

What makes our faith strong enough to withstand terrible temptation and fear?

future so that our past does not overwhelm us. God comes to give us hope in life-giving relationships that have a future. God comes to teach and model for us, through the "hands-on" Emmanuel, how to live in relationship with one another and in obedience to God. Matthew's Gospel is about Emmanuel, God with us, in relationship with us.

Therefore it is not surprising that among the first characters we meet in the Gospel are the magi from an unnamed country in "the East" (2:1-12). The story of the magi appears only in Matthew, and hence we can hear Matthew speaking in the Christmas hymn of "We Three Kings" as well as in gift shops where wise men figurines continue to inspire many. Indeed, Matthew's story of the wise men bringing gifts has hit a core of who we are, and both the believer and the nonbeliever alike have continued to emulate these wise ones with gift-giving at Christmas. These characters are different, and their differences are affirmed by Matthew.

Unlike the tradition of heeding prophecies, the wise ones are different because they observe stars and follow the star. This comes as quite a surprise. Religious outsiders, whom some might consider pagan, decipher God's fullness and come to worship. The Christ event is not limited to a few. God's promise invades even cultures and peoples that we would count as outsiders.

On the other hand, the insiders who have the prophecy before their eyes are unable to decipher what it means. When King Herod summons his priests and scribes, these "insiders" seem to have the information that the Messiah would be born "in Bethlehem of Judea" as it had been prophesied (2:5). Yet their information is useless. They are not able to decipher the events.

In the story of the magi, Matthew begins to gather unusual people around Jesus, even people who practice unusual customs such as reading stars and who come from places so far away that they are only known as "the

Read Matthew 2:1-12. What do you know about the wise men that is actually biblical? What contribution does the report of this visit make to the Jesus story when we consider that the magi were Gentiles?

How do you interpret the "insider" and "outsider" positions regarding those who are concerned with the coming of a Messiah? Have you ever been so close to a situation that you could not see what was unfolding before you? Is it possible to miss the action of God in history by being too far inside or outside? Explain.

MATTHEW'S MESSAGE

East." Once again we see the beginnings of "many will come from east and west and will eat" at God's table (8:11).

Recognizing the Kingdom

Matthew encourages us to pay attention to the inbreakings of the kingdom of heaven in our world and in our daily lives. This can be a bit of a challenge, especially when we expect the kingdom of heaven to be so differently Other. When it comes, it is so simple, so natural, and at times so small that we do not always see it.

The Kingdom parables Matthew records work to surprise us. Matthew tells us the kingdom of heaven is like a mustard seed (13:31-32) or like yeast (13:33). The kingdom of heaven has small beginnings, takes time, and is so natural in some ways. Perhaps the danger of being blind to the presence of the kingdom of heaven is in the familiarity. We therefore might miss the miracle of the mustard seed by being so accustomed to the large tree it has become. Or we might miss the strange ways of yeast by being accustomed to our daily bread. In the same way, we might miss the inbreaking of the kingdom of heaven around us because we expect something very Other.

There is, in fact, an "otherly" quality about the Kingdom. We refer again to Jesus' affirmation and inclusion of those who are "different." Matthew reports among Jesus' Kingdom parables that the "kingdom of heaven is like a net that was thrown into the sea and caught fish of every kind" (13:47-50). The parable goes on to explain that those "fish" will be sorted out (as will the "sheep" and the "goats" in Matthew 25:31-46). The good will be separated from the evil, and each will receive the appropriate eternal reward. Still, "fish" of every kind are evaluated according to their goodness or faithfulness, not according to their "fishiness."

This story reminds us of the catch of 153 fish that Peter hauled in (John 21:9-11), a reference that may imply that every

Review Matthew 13:31-33. How, do you think, is the Kingdom like these small, ordinary things? With what might you compare the Kingdom today? Why?

Read Matthew 13:47-50 and John 21:9-11. How do you interpret the "fish" and the "net"? What are the "fish of every kind"? Do you consider yourself among the "fish"? Explain. Compare this passage with Matthew 25:31-46. What are the criteria for judgment?

known kind of "fish"—the fullness of human culture and variety—would be caught by Jesus' heavenly "net."

Contemporary Signs of the Kingdom

Jesus' net casts far and wide, as we witness the work of the Holy Spirit in ways we thought we would never see. As we exit the second millennium, we can count how fortunate we have been to witness the collapse of the Berlin wall and the collapse of apartheid in our lifetime. We are encouraged and empowered by the lives of men such as Nelson Mandela who survived twenty-seven years of banishment by a white government. Mandela emerged from prison to become president of South Africa, still determined about the future.

In spite of being born and growing up in apartheid—a legal system of separation that kept persons apart racially and theologically—Mandela dared to see a different future for his country than the one painted by apartheid. For one born into such a system, one solution would be to do right by the system and stay out of trouble. Or perhaps a black person born into such a system could grow to justifiably hate white people. Or perhaps one could immigrate to another country, and indeed many took that option for themselves and for their families.

But Mandela's vision of a new future for his country dared him in 1962 to say, "I detest racialism because I regard it as a barbaric thing, whether it comes from a white man or whether it comes from a black man."

In the famous Rivornia trial in 1962, Mandela said these words: "I have fought against white domination, and I have fought against black domination. I have cherished the ideal of a democratic and free society in which all persons live together in harmony and with equal opportunities. It is an ideal which I hope to live for and to achieve. But if needs be, it is an ideal for which I am prepared to die." One of the foundations of

Do you remember the building of the Berlin Wall? the destruction of the wall? the imprisonment of Nelson Mandela? his release? If so, what do you remember; and how do you think these events have colored human affairs? What is the most transformational event in your own lifetime? Why does it have such power for you?

How do you think a Kingdom vision of the future has influenced global leaders? their nations? What is your vision of the future? Does it include the work of the Spirit? Explain.

MATTHEW'S MESSAGE

a vision of the Kingdom is the promise that God will vindicate the faithful.

"Unlearning Privilege"

Matthew had a vision for such a world but more so: he saw a world rooted in radical discipleship. For Matthew, the key was in relationships with people who are different. But it is more than just a friendly relationship. It is a relationship of learning to speak so that the other person can take us seriously and engage us in dialogue or conversation. It is a relationship where the other person is able to talk back.

In such relationships the challenge is to unlearn privilege. That is, we are no longer to consciously or unconsciously assume we have some rights that another person does not have. Unlearning privilege means shifting from self-preoccupation into attentiveness to how those who are different from us are being treated. Of course, attentiveness is not enough. Leaving behind the assumptions and observing carefully is a beginning, but true discipleship results when our attention moves us to action that brings justice for everyone, regardless of class or station in life.

In Matthew's Gospel we constantly meet models of these kinds of experiences. Our best model is, of course, Jesus himself. Jesus is often in dialogue with the most unexpected people. Jesus meets two blind men on two occasions (9:27-31; 20:29-34). Although these blind men call out for healing, Jesus does not immediately heal them. He dialogues with them. "Do you believe that I am able to do this?" he asks (9:28) and more pointedly, "What do you want me do for you?"

Do you believe that God will vindicate the faithful? Explain.

What does "unlearning privilege" mean to you? Do you have any privilege? If so, what is it? Do you need to reevaluate how you use your privileges? What would be a Kingdom view of privilege?

Read Matthew 9:27-31. Does their belief, do you think, in Jesus' capabilities somehow enable Jesus to heal them?

Read Matthew 20:29-34 and compare it with Matthew 9:27-31. What are the implications for these men of being able to see again? Does Jesus ever ask you what he can do for you? How? What would you like Jesus to do for you and what would be the consequences if he did it?

(20:32). Jesus' conversation first elicits the felt need and expectations. He then goes beyond what could be regarded as the quick fix, an immediate healing.

Jesus' question penetrates layers of perceived needs and pushes the men to consider all the implications of what they ask of him. In effect, they are brought in as associates in their own healing because they are given the opportunity to evaluate the consequences of what a healing would accomplish and to determine if that is what they truly want. Jesus not only heals, he empowers the men.

When Jesus encounters the Canaanite woman, the story moves with dialogue and hesitancy until Jesus and the woman arrive at a new relationship (15:21-28). The Canaanite woman makes a claim for God's abundant mercy whose surplus falls even on those who had not been initially included. Again, the model of who is "supposed" to have privilege and those who receive Jesus' care is turned upside down.

Including Rome

Another surprising relationship in Matthew's Gospel is the inclusion of two centurions in the new community (8:5-13; 27:54). Since Matthew lived with the backdrop of the Roman Empire, the inclusion of Roman soldiers in the new community is challenging. The Romans were the super-power of the day as well being arrogant colonizers. They insisted that colonized people adopt the Greco-Roman way.

Judea was a Roman province under a Roman governor. Roman domination frustrated the people of Palestine and their hopes of speedy deliverance from Roman domination. The period has much literature of prophetic sermons and apocalyptic literature predicting that the Jews would overcome

The Canaanite woman is not the only mother who intercedes for her child in the Gospel of Matthew. Just before entering Jerusalem, the mother of James and John approached Jesus on their behalf and asked for special privilege. Unlike the Canaanite woman, who was an outsider, the disciples were insiders. Compare Matthew 15:21-28 with Matthew 20:20-28. Are parents always wise about what their children need?

Review these two passages about the centurions (or possibly the same centurion). What do these passages teach about power and authority? How does the Gospel of Matthew turn upside down traditional notions of power and authority?

Rome under a Messiah who would arrive soon.

Matthew's account of a military officer who is without power is surprising. The account is about reaching the limits of power even for those who are so oppressively powerful and inaccessible. Therefore the presence of a Roman military officer should take us aback (8:5-13). This particular centurion is a man with authority and claims that he is "a man under authority, with soldiers under me; and I say to one, 'Go,' and he goes, and to another, 'Come,' and he comes, and to my slave, 'Do this,' and the slave does it" (8:9). The centurion has not come to plead for himself but for his slave who is ill.

We do not know if the servant has any faith in Jesus; but like the Canaanite woman, the centurion comes to intercede. Is this compassion on his part, or is he simply interested in getting his property (servant) repaired for use? It is not an easy speculation. I would like to imagine the officer was a man of compassion because he reports to Jesus the state of his slave: "Lord, my servant is lying at home paralyzed, in terrible distress" (8:6). His servant's distress, therefore, rather than his servant's inability to work, might have moved him to seek help.

I also need to believe in the compassion of this centurion because the story then becomes healing for me in my encounter with those whom I see now as "centurions" in their power to oppress others. The centurion's presence in the account moves us from demonizing the Romans into a personal encounter with one Roman. In this encounter, he is stripped of his power to make things happen with simply a word (8:9). The Roman officer confesses that in spite of his authority, he is impotent to help one who is even more powerless than he, his servant.

From Relationship to Discipleship

Matthew reminds us to keep our eyes on what is important lest the trivial things overwhelm our Christian discipleship. Matthew keeps us centered in the good news of Jesus Messiah. In the Gospel of Matthew, God has come to be with us in the birth,

When have you seen compassion from "centurions," those persons you expect not to care or to help?

What are the trivial things that interfere with your own active discipleship? What can you do about it? What prevents you from doing anything about it?

life, and passion of Jesus Christ. The name *Jesus* is the clue. Matthew translates for us the meaning of *Jesus* as "he will save his people from their sins" (1:21). *Jesus* is not a name that is new for Matthew. *Jesus* is a name taken from the Old Testament Hebrew name "Joshua," which means "God saves" or "God helps." Jesus is also named "Emmanuel," which means "God is with us" (1:23). *Emmanuel* is not a name that is new with Matthew. *Emmanuel* is a name taken from the prophet Isaiah's prophecy: "Look, the young woman is with child and shall bear a son, and shall name him Immanuel" (Isaiah 7:14). Matthew begins his Gospel by announcing the good news of God's saving presence in Jesus Christ (Matthew 1:21-23). Matthew ends his Gospel with Jesus announcing the good news, saying, "Remember, I am with you always, to the end of the age" (28:20).

According to Matthew, our future is not about conquering our past or reversing our history or erasing our traditions and languages. Matthew saw a new community that dared to live in radical ways that overcome the ghosts of our past. Matthew saw a community that dared to believe in the justice and mercy of God for all. When Matthew speaks to us today, Matthew dares us to trust God and to live the gospel in radical ways. Matthew dares us to put all our eggs in God's basket; to risk it all for the kingdom of heaven; to throw away any alternative plan! If necessary we are to sell everything we own, give up everything we ever had, and stake our lives on the gospel.

The Call of the Future

The churches of the United States and elsewhere face the challenges of the current days and the third millennium as they have to prove their relevance to a post-modern generation. No longer can we take for granted that the church is an institution honored by the majority. No longer can we assume that the same models of ministry will work in the cyber-

---

In the Bible, names are often descriptive of a relationship; a personal characteristic; or a special event, particularly with God. How do we name or acknowledge transformational events or special people?

What have you gleaned from Matthew about the future of the global church? your own church? your own future?

What, do you think, are the challenges facing the global church and your church?

---

age. Indeed, in an era in which we have progressed from traveling by foot to trekking among the stars, most of the world's citizens have witnessed a paradigm shift of epoch proportions.

For African Christians, it means we can no longer mimic other Christians in other places. We can no longer invest in the middleman. We are called out of the tragic habit of maintaining church for the sake of having a church and into the business of building the church of the future. This church must take seriously the context and search persistently for new ways; new structures; new concepts; new theologies; new language; new metaphors to speak directly, clearly, and meaningfully about God. We have to get new wineskins for this new thing God is doing. There is no way the old skins can hold the new wine. We have to get new garments for this new thing God is doing. The patched garments can no longer hold the thriving, live body of Christ (9:16-17).

The excitement is sometimes overwhelming when we catch a glimpse of God's church of the future that is African culturally, spiritually, morally, physically; a church of the future where the gospel runs deeper than the bones of our differences.

The third millennium is fertile ground for such a community.

What traditions do you follow in your church or family that may actually now be "ruts"—practices or rituals that no longer hold the same meaning or that no longer work? Should they be changed? Explain. If so, what might fruitfully take their place?

What is the newest "wineskin" in your church or in your own life? What has been the consequence? What has been the benefit? the downside?

What new things do you think God is doing as we face a new millennium? What new wineskins do you think we need, and where might we find them?

Jesus Messiah calls each of us to a radical discipleship. What do you think God is calling you to do? Take a moment in prayer to ask God about that call and to commit or recommit your life to Christ.

MATTHEW LOOKS AT THE NEW MILLENNIUM

Ready or not, the third millennium is upon us. While much has been made of the preparation for this new era, at least a few important things need extra help to be ready for the third millennium.

The Great "00" Dilemma

We are all aware of the general alarm raised over the Y2K problem, the programming conundrum caused when computers fail to recognize the third millennium dates as a new, rather than a prior, century. All kinds of date-sensitive equipment and gadgets are affected by the turn of the new millennium. The problem is global and dynamic; systems all over the world are interconnected and are, in spite of their sophistication, rather fragile. A glitch in one part of one system can cascade into thousands of problems throughout these global networks.

Reprogramming millions of computers is a massive undertaking. Though it will not change the fundamentals of the equipment, it will give the computers the ability to recognize a new date system.

News of the magnitude of this situation has opened up a whole barrage of reflection and discussion. One response is panic; people "heading to the hills" to hide out before and until the malfunctioning computers are fixed, thus fending off any potential hazards. Another response is excitement and suspicion. Perhaps recent computers were deliberately made without the "millennium chips" in order to spark a sales and repair boom for the industry. Think of the nearly boundless entrepreneurial opportunities for those who know how to address the corrections and the systems and the myriad of ways crooks and hackers will find to exploit

How do you respond to major changes? Do you think the new millennium will require you to change in any significant way? If so, how?

and prey upon the fears and insecurities of others.

Matthew's church is a helpful church for us at the opening of the third millennium because it too included all these catetories of people—the fearful and the excited, the suspicious and the helpful, the scam artist and the expert. The bottom line is that Matthew's Gospel encourages us to live in anticipation of something new when we live in God's will.

Awesome, Alarming, and Exhilarating

Matthew's Gospel prepares Christians for the awesome, alarming, and exhilarating challenge of the third millennium. I would not be surprised if Christians who lived in past centuries would envy us such a phenomenal time to be alive. God seems to have especially favored us with the joy and responsibility of living smack in the middle of a major fulfillment of the community Matthew's Gospel had made a witness to! Once again the words of Jesus echo true that "many prophets and righteous people longed to see what you see, but did not see it, and to hear what you hear, but did not hear it" (13:17). Third-millennium Christians are in an unusual place because the tools of the past are not able to serve our new situation. Old paradigms have cracked under the pressure, and the jury is still out on the new possibilities.

We now consider intolerable the clichés and stereotypes about people who are different from us, such as "noble savages." It is now beyond question that people come in a wide variety of cultures, colors, shapes, and accents. Patriarchy is tottering in many parts of our world. Great strides have been made in redefining terms of relationships for women, people of color, and creation. Empires have loosened their deathly grip on faraway lands, and more natives are finally finding voice and speaking up. We are no longer looking for ways of conquering and dominating.

We are now in the business of listening for God's word for our situation and living in obedience to that word. The third millen-

Read Matthew 13:14-17. What do you think this passage means? What do you hear or see from the Gospel that others seem not to hear or see?

What major cultural or sociological shifts have you observed in your lifetime? What shifts in religious practice? What major shifts of perception have you made?

MATTHEW'S MESSAGE

nium is a wonderful time to be alive and, more so, to be a Christian.

A Common Ground

If Matthew were alive today, he would fit right in our situations. If anything would surprise him, it would most likely be the common ground we share in our hopes and fears, anxieties and dilemmas. Matthew would be familiar with the flux of the world around us as the third millennium begins. Matthew would be familiar with the inability of old paradigms to cope with the new existence God is bringing into being. Matthew would be familiar with our furious attempts to salvage yesterday's familiarity and patch it up so it can cope with a new day. Matthew hits the nail on the head when he comments on the futility of putting new wine in old wineskins or attempting to patch up an old garment with a new, unshrunk piece of cloth. The damage done in both cases makes the situation worse (9:16-17). In spite of common ground, the Gospel calls us to a new day, complete with its own set of problems and issues (6:31-34). In seeking the King-

dom and trusting in God, each day's dilemmas are not ignored, but are sufficiently addressed.

The Dilemma of Divisive Traditions

Matthew's first major dilemma involved a traditional, cultural issue that had evolved into a religious and ethical standard—circumcision. Strangely enough, although the origins of this rite are not clear, the Hebrews had come to view circumcision as a mark of God's chosen people. The divine demand for circumcision was traced to Abraham (Genesis 17:9-27). The rite was interpreted theologically and guarded as a sign of the covenant people. No wonder there had been riots and revolts when anti-Jewish emperors and culture had either banned or ridiculed circumcision. No wonder the neighboring Edomites and Idumeans were forcibly circumcised by the Jewish Hasmoneans who conquered and attempted to assimilate them.

As Matthew nurtured a predominantly Jewish-Christian church into accepting Gentile Christians, the question of circumcision was first and foremost in the minds of Jewish believers.

Read Matthew 6:25-34. What does this passage mean to you? Do you have a secure sense that God will provide? What troubles are enough for today? Should people of faith have any worry for tomorrow? Explain.

As it was, the rift between the synagogue and the church was widening. Where synagogue and church relationships were concerned, it was clear that circumcision was a proverbial straw that would break the camel's back beyond repair.

If Matthew's congregation accepted uncircumcised Gentiles into fellowship, it would be a sure departure from fellowship with what it traditionally meant to be a Jew grounded in Hebrew Scriptures. It was an emotive issue and impossible for many devoted Jewish believers. How does one separate such an ancient tradition with what it means to live a righteousness life and to be obedient to God?

The traditional belief system made it impossible to comprehend the uncircumcised as full and respectable members of God's people. The only solution seemed to be to circumcise Gentiles who converted. Many opted for this easier solution. But not Matthew. Matthew's church was radical and visionary when it became the first Christian community to accept Gentiles into full fellowship without requiring circumcision. For Matthew, it was clear where tradition gave way to the good news of the kingdom of heaven.

The good news was not about becoming a Jew. The good news was about living a righteous and obedient life. For Matthew, the marks of discipleship were not in the physical and cultural customs but in obedience to God and in righteous living in community. Imagine how radical that must have been. Imagine how many of the circumcised were upset, disgusted, and downright furious. Imagine the pressure Matthew took in order for people like you and me to belong. Matthew was extraordinary!

The Dilemma of Conflict Over the Temple

Matthew's second dilemma concerned the Temple. Quite likely, Matthew was familiar with the

Using a Bible dictionary, explore the act of circumcision as a sign of covenant. What are the signs of our covenants in the faith community now? What traditions remain strong in the faith community? What traditions in our church no longer have the same significance as they once did?

How would you define the marks of discipleship for our day? Are any of these marks a response to the current demands of our society as it is today? What circumstances require us to define our standards in any age?

destruction in A.D. 70 of the Temple, which had been the center for worship and political life. It was impossible for many to fathom life without the Temple. Matthew records Jesus' intense conflict with the Temple officials (Matthew 21–23).

One of the ways Matthew especially underlines the conflict with the Temple is by making it the first place Jesus entered on his final visit to Jerusalem. The incident is not only memorable because it is Jesus' first stop in Jerusalem but also because the conflict is physical and violent. Many an artist has painted Jesus turning over the money changers' tables and seats and creating havoc by letting loose the doves (21:12). Many Bibles title this scenario "Cleansing of the Temple."

Later when the disciples had perhaps pointed out to Jesus the beauty, the security, and maybe even the secure moorings of the building, we realize that for all its obvious physical attributes, the Temple was not the center of strength. The disciples must have been astonished when Jesus predicted that "not one stone will be left here upon another; all will be thrown down" (24:2).

As we face the post-modern third millennium, we also realize that the temple, the church, the kingdom hall, the synagogue, are not such central places as they once were. Ironically, we are entering an age in which our spiritual hunger seems to be great and largely unsatisfied, while in many societies our trust in and reliance on the institutions of faith and worship are at a critical ebb. Though the Temple building fall, Matthew tells us, the Son of Man and his angels will gather the faithful "from one end of heaven to the other" (24:30-31); and he will be with us all daily until the end of the age. Therein lies hope for a new millennium.

The Dilemma of Fragmentation

A third dilemma for Matthew was how peoples who had been previously separated and hostile to

Review Matthew 21–23. What was the nature of Jesus' controversy and confrontation with religious leaders of his day? What current circumstances today seem equivalent? What do you think Jesus would do today?

How do we cope today with the erosion of respect for and reliance on the institutional church in some societies? What institutions, if any, of your culture are under fire? What are the implications of reexamining or challenging those institutions?

one another would forge healing relationships in the new community gathered around Jesus Messiah. Matthew was calling for a reordering of a future together in spite of a messy history of fragmentation.

In this reordering of history, the story of the Canaanite woman in Matthew 15:21-28 becomes pivotal. The mother of a sick child unexpectedly reorders the history between Israel and its enemies by claiming God's mercy even for those who were previously excluded.

The story has another level; the woman is at a disadvantage because she is not an Israelite. Worse still she is not just a "mere Gentile," but a Canaanite. This identification is important because of the load of historical baggage of hostile racial and ethnic relations.

Canaan was the ancient name of the territory that included ancient Palestine, land already inhabited when the Israelites entered the Promised Land. The two ethnic groups were extremely hostile to each other; and tensions were extended into cultural, religious, and political arenas. The Israelites loathed the Canaanites and considered them, their religion, and their ways of life inferior and an abomination. Genesis 9:18-27 records that Canaan, the grandson of Noah, is cursed and made "a slave to his brothers." Israel's literature urged the eradication of Canaanite people and religion altogether and found theological grounds for this genocide (Deuteronomy 20:16-18).

The woman is therefore not just a non-Israelite or a "regular" Gentile; she is from anti-Israelite stock. In light of this history of antagonism, the appearance of the Canaanite woman in the Gospel of Matthew is both unexpected and rather startling.

The Canaanite woman enters the Gospel of Matthew because she is a mother whose child is sick. She has come to plead for her demon-possessed daughter. This mother's desperation for her child transcends ethnic and cultural walls. This mother is not shy; she is so obnoxious with her shouting that she disturbs the disciples (Matthew 15:23).

Read Matthew 15:21-28, and study it further using a Bible commentary. What are the surprises or ironies in this story for you? (Check on Genesis 9:18-27 and Deuteronomy 20:16-18 for more background.)

What does the Canaanite woman do to get Jesus' attention, and how do he and his party respond? Have you ever "sparred" with Jesus in prayer? What happened?

The disciples cannot stand her shouting and plead with Jesus to grant her what she wishes in order to get rid of her. The Canaanite woman calls to Jesus using his titles of "Lord" and "Son of David," pleading, "Have mercy on me, Lord, Son of David" and "Lord, help me" (15:22, 25). Jesus at first does not answer her. Instead he reminds the disciples that his boundaries of mission are limited to the house of Israel. In other words, she is out of his jurisdiction.

But the woman will have none of that. She pushes against the ethnic, religious, and mission boundaries, kneeling before Jesus and pleading, "Lord, help me." Finally, she is in his face; and he cannot ignore her.

Jesus at first demurs; she is not among the first priority group of his mission. The derogatory reference to the distasteful Canaanites as dogs sounds shocking and rude but does not deter her. She pushes Jesus' metaphor further, using her common wisdom to request "the crumbs that fall from [the master's] table." She makes a claim for God's abundant mercy whose surplus falls even on those who had not been initially included.

If there was a time for the Gospel to record Jesus' surprise and appreciation of common-sense insight that carries faith, this could be it. Jesus cannot deny her mercy. Saying, "let it be done for you as you wish," he grants her not just the limited healing of her daughter but her heart's desire (15:28).

It is likewise the heart's desire of common folk of every age to find peace and healing, and the world is still a decidedly fragmented place. Matthew would teach us that for a new millennium, the desperate call of mothers for the healing of their loved one is an urgent but a reachable one. The undulating processes of peace in, for example, the Middle East, Ireland, Africa, may lurch along with shocking and rude detours born of animosity and extremist attitudes. But the pleading of the family of God to Jesus Messiah, "Lord, help me," will certainly be heard.

The Dilemma of Creating Family

Matthew's fourth dilemma was on how to be family. We meet unusual families in Matthew's Gospel. The Canaanite woman is

What do you think it means to gain your heart's desire through supplication to Jesus Messiah? Have you ever asked for help from God and received it? apparently not received it? Describe one experience and what it meant to you.

not the only mother who intercedes for her child in the Gospel of Matthew. The mother of James and John approaches Jesus and asks for privilege for her sons (20:20-28). Unlike the Canaanite woman who was an outsider, the disciples were insiders. Their mother wished for them to attain an even higher status and closer relationship to the source of power. She therefore pleaded for her sons to sit on the right and the left of Jesus' throne in his kingdom. Jesus corrected her by reminding her that the relationship in the kingdom of heaven is one of service and not privilege (20:26-28).

In another teaching moment, Jesus reminds us that faithful service may crash head to head with family. In an ominous comment on the cost of discipleship, he warned that loving father or mother, son or daughter more than loving him casts doubt on the integrity of one's commitment (10:34-39). Jesus' ministry may cause dissension within the family if not all of its members accept the radical message of commitment and reconciliation. Jesus Messiah, who calls us to forgive our "brother" seventy-seven times (18:21-22), calls us at the advent of the third millennium to lay down the sword in families, in relationships, and with our global family.

The Call for Prayer

The relationship that Jesus is calling the new community to forge is one that is as difficult as moving mountains and can be achieved only by faith (17:20)

Read Matthew 20:20-28. What was the mother asking? Was the request reasonable to Jesus? Did he grant it? In what ways do we ask the same question in our own time? How do you think Jesus Messiah responds?

Read Matthew 10:34-39. What are the issues and costs of discipleship and the implications for one's family? Did Jesus literally mean that he would deliberately come between family members or that we are unworthy if we love our family? What is the message of discipleship in this passage? Can you accept it? Explain.

Radical discipleship also requires radical forgiveness. Read Matthew 18:15-22. What does this passage teach about support and accountability for those in the faith community? Do we have the same responsibilities for forgiveness with those outside the faith community? Explain.

and by prayer. In Matthew, Jesus teaches us how to pray.

On the one hand prayer is private; Jesus says "go into your room and shut the door and pray to your Father who is in secret" (6:6). On the other hand, in prayer we are always to be located in community. Therefore, we pray to "Our Father in heaven" (6:9) and not to "My father."

In prayer we find the space we need daily to renew our allegiance to God (6:10) and to recommit ourselves into living in community with others (6:12, 14). Jesus modeled both personal and community prayer for us when in Gethsemane he prayed for God's will to be done (26:39, 42). Despite his distress, Jesus was focused on obedience to God.

Jesus asked Peter and the two sons of Zebedee to accompany him (26:37). His sleepy disciples found it difficult to stay awake and "pray that you may not come into the time of trial" (26:41). Thus being ill-equipped when the time of trial was suddenly upon them, they "deserted him and fled" (26:56). Jesus teaches us to pray, not so that we will not suffer, but so that we can make it through in spite of the suffering.

Looking Forward

In spite of the suffering, the church of Jesus Christ survives and enters its third millennium. In a way, if Matthew's church was beginning the journey as the new community of Jesus, our third millennium church has traveled quite a distance into what seemed like the horizon for Matthew. If Matthew's church was more romantic with a clean canvas and a fresh start as God's faithful people, the third millennium church has lived and battled a history that often appears to be the very thing Matthew had hoped we would not become. If Matthew's world was one of nurturing the mustard seed, the third-millennium church is still nurturing mustard seeds in some places even while in other places it is involved in the task of pruning and making hospitable "the greatest of shrubs" so that the birds of the air can find a place to nest (13:32).

Our times may be very dif-

Examine Jesus' teaching about prayer in Matthew 6:5-16. How is this both personal and corporate? How do you experience prayer?

Review Matthew 26:36-46. How did Jesus' experience of prayer in Gethsemane prepare him for what he was about to face? How did the disciples fare? Does prayer prepare you to face difficulties? Explain.

ferent from Matthew's time, but the demands his Gospel makes on Christians have not changed. Just like first-century followers of Jesus, we are called to live in relationships of justice and mercy with our neighbors and in obedience to God. Our third-millennium challenge is to retell the story of Jesus in terms of our experiences, events, and history in order to dare see how God fulfills the promise even in our times. Matthew gives us permission to be a confessing and testifying church where our stories of encounter with Jesus are told and retold.

What do you see as the challenges facing Christians at the brink of a new millennium? facing you? What can the church do to address those challenges? What can you do?

Having concluded your study of Matthew, review the teachings of this Gospel. Take time in prayer to commit or to recommit yourself to Jesus Messiah and think about how to share this Gospel with others.

52994494R00041

Made in the USA
Columbia, SC
09 March 2019